THE DAILY STUDY BIBLE

THE LETTERS TO
THE GALATIANS AND EPHESIANS

K—1

THE LETTER TO
THE GALATIANS

The Rev. WILLIAM BARCLAY, D.D.

Lecturer in New Testament Language and Literature and in Hellenistic Greek in the University of Glasgow

THE SAINT ANDREW PRESS
EDINBURGH

Published by The Saint Andrew Press
121 George Street, Edinburgh, 2
and printed in Scotland by
McCorquodale & Co., Ltd., Glasgow

First Edition   -   May, 1954
Second Edition   -   September, 1958
Second Impression -   November, 1960

To G. A. M.
TO ME A FATHER IN GOD,
WHO FIRST GAVE ME THE OPPORTUNITY TO WRITE A BOOK,
WHOSE ENCOURAGEMENT
HAS OFTEN COMPELLED ME TO GO ON
WHEN OTHERWISE I WOULD HAVE GIVEN UP,
WHOSE GUIDANCE HAS SAVED ME FROM MANY A MISTAKE,
AND WHOSE WISDOM HAS SAVED ME
FROM MANY A HERESY,
AND TO WHOM I OWE MORE THAN I CAN EVER REPAY.

GENERAL INTRODUCTION

IT may truly be said that this series of Daily Bible Studies began almost accidentally. A series which the Church of Scotland was using came to an end, and another series was immediately required. I was asked to write a volume on *Acts*, and, at the moment, had no intention beyond that. But one volume followed another, until the demand for one volume became a plan to write on the whole New Testament.

The translation which is given in each volume claims no special merit. It was included in order that the reader might be able to carry both the text of the New Testament and the comments on it wherever he went, and that he might be able to read it anywhere. While I was making the translation, the translations of Moffatt, Weymouth, and Knox were ever beside me. *The American Revised Standard Version, The Twentieth Century New Testament*, and *The New Testament in Plain English*, by Charles Kingsley Williams, have been in constant use. Since its publication, I have consistently consulted *The Authentic New Testament*, translated by Hugh J. Schonfield.

I cannot see another edition of these books going out to the public without expressing my very deep and sincere gratitude to the Church of Scotland Publications Committee for allowing me the privilege of first beginning, and then continuing, this series. And in particular I wish to express my very great gratitude to the convener, Rev. R. G. Macdonald, O.B.E., M.A., D.D., and to the committee's secretary and manager, Rev. Andrew McCosh, M.A., S.T.M., for constant encouragement and never-failing sympathy and help.

As these volumes went on, the idea of the whole series developed. The aim is to make the results of modern scholarship available to the non-technical reader in a form that it does not require a theological education to understand; and then to seek to make the teaching of the New Testament books relevant to life and work to-day. The whole aim of these books is summed up in Richard of Chichester's famous prayer; they are meant to enable men and women to know Jesus Christ more clearly, to love Him more dearly, and to follow Him more nearly. It is my prayer that they may do something to make that possible.

LETTERS TO THE GALATIANS AND EPHESIANS

CONTENTS

LETTERS TO THE GALATIANS AND EPHESIANS

CONTENTS

CONTENTS

FOREWORD TO GALATIANS

IT is but natural that a book which has had the influence on the Church that *Galatians* has had should have had many commentators. He who would write on *Galatians*, and he who would study it has a wealth of material on which to draw.

One of Luther's greatest works is his *Commentary on Galatians*. J. B. Lightfoot's commentary can never be superseded. The commentary of E. D. Burton in the International Critical Commentary is a monument of patient scholarship and a treasure-house of material.

On the English text the commentary of A. W. F. Blunt in the Clarendon Bible is good; but the best English commentary remains that of G. S. Duncan in the *Moffatt Commentary*.

There is no letter which takes us nearer to the heart of Paul's gospel than *Galatians* does, and it is my hope that this little volume on it will do something to make it more real and intelligible to us.

WILLIAM BARCLAY.

TRINITY COLLEGE,
   GLASGOW.
      September, 1958.

A GENERAL INTRODUCTION TO THE LETTERS
OF PAUL

The Letters of Paul

There is no more interesting body of documents in the New Testament than the letters of Paul. That is so because of all forms of literature a letter is most personal. Demetrius, one of the old Greek literary critics, once wrote, " Every one reveals his own soul in his letters. In every other form of composition it is possible to discern the writer's character, but in none so clearly as the epistolary." (Demetrius, *On Style*, 227). It is just because he left us so many letters that we feel we know Paul so well. In these letters he opened his mind and heart to the folk he loved so much; and in them, to this day, we can see that great mind grappling with the problems of the Early Church, and we can feel that great heart throbbing with love for men, even when they were misguided and mistaken.

The Difficulty of Letters

And yet, at the same time, it remains true that there is often nothing so difficult to understand as a letter. Demetrius (*On Style*, 223) quotes a saying of Artemon, who edited the letters of Aristotle. Artemon said that a letter ought to be written in the same manner as a dialogue, because he regarded a letter as one of the two sides of a dialogue. To put it in a more modern way, to read a letter is like listening to one side of a telephone conversation. So when we read the letters of Paul we are often in a difficulty. We do not possess the letter which he was answering; we do not fully know the circumstances with which he was dealing; it is only from the letter that we can deduce the situation which prompted the letter. Always, in reading these letters, we are presented with a double problem. There is the problem of understanding the letter, and there is the prior problem that we will not fully understand the letter itself unless we understand the situation which was the moving cause for the sake of which the letter was written. We have continuously to seek to reconstruct the situation against which the letter is to be read.

The Ancient Letters

It is a great pity that Paul's letters were ever called *epistles*. They are in the most literal sense *letters*. One of the great lights on the interpretation of the New Testament has been the discovery and the publication of the *papyri*. In the ancient world, *papyrus* was the substance on which most documents were written. It was composed of strips of the pith of a certain bulrush that grew on the banks of the Nile. These strips were laid one on the top of the other to form a substance very like brown paper. The sands of the Egyptian desert were ideal for the preservation of these papyri, for papyrus, although it is very brittle, will last forever so long as moisture does not get at it. So from the Egyptian rubbish heaps archaeologists have rescued literally hundreds of documents, marriage contracts, legal agreements, government forms, and, most interesting of all, hundreds of private letters. When we read these private letters we find that there was a pattern to which nearly all letters conformed; and we find that the letters of Paul reproduce exactly and precisely the pattern of the letters which people in the ancient world wrote to each other every day. Here is one of these ancient letters. It is from a soldier, called Apion, to his father Epimachus. He was writing from Misenum to tell his father that he had arrived safely after a stormy passage.

" Apion sends heartiest greetings to his father and lord
Epimachus. I pray above all that you are well and
fit; and that things are going well with you and my
sister and her daughter and my brother. I thank
my Lord Serapis (his god) that he kept me safe when
I was in peril on the sea. As soon as I got to Misenum
I got my journey money from Caesar—three gold
pieces. And things are going fine with me. So I
beg you, my dear father, send me a line, first to let
me know how you are, and then about my brothers,
and thirdly, that I may kiss your hand, because
you brought me up well, and because of that, I hope,
God willing, soon to be promoted. Give Capito my
heartiest greetings, and my brothers and Serenilla
and my friends. I sent you a little picture of myself
painted by Euctemon. My military name is Antonius
Maximus. I pray for your good health. Serenus
sends good wishes, Agathos Daimon's boy, and
Turbo, Gallonius' son." (G. Milligan, *Selections from
the Greek Papyri*, 36).

Little did Apion think that we would be reading his letter
to his father 1800 years after he had written it. It shows
how little human nature changes. The lad is hoping for
promotion quickly. Who will Serenilla be but the girl
he left behind him? He sends the ancient equivalent of
a photograph to the folk at home. Now that letter falls
into certain sections. (i) There is a greeting. (ii) There is
a prayer for the health of the recipients. (iii) There is
a thanksgiving to the gods. (iv) There are the special
contents. (v) Finally, there are the special salutations
and the personal greetings. Practically every one of Paul's
letters shows exactly the same sections. Let us apply
these sections to Paul's letters.

(i) *The Greeting:* Romans I: I; I Corinthians I: I;
2 Corinthians I: I; Galatians I: I; Ephesians I: I;
Philippians I: I; Colossians I: I, 2; I Thessalonians
I: I; 2 Thessalonians I: I.

(ii) *The Prayer:* in every case Paul prays for the grace of God on the people to whom he writes: Romans 1: 7; 1 Corinthians 1: 3; 2 Corinthians 1: 2; Galatians 1: 3; Ephesians 1: 2; Philippians 1: 3; Colossians 1: 2; 1 Thessalonians 1: 1; 2 Thessalonians 1: 2.

(iii) *The Thanksgiving:* Romans 1: 8; 1 Corinthians 1: 4; 2 Corinthians 1: 3; Ephesians 1: 3; Philippians 1: 3; 1 Thessalonians 1: 3; 2 Thessalonians 1: 3.

(iv) *The Special Contents:* the main body of the letter contains the special contents.

(v) *Special Salutations and Personal Greetings:* Romans 16; 1 Corinthians 16: 19; 2 Corinthians 13: 13; Philippians 4: 21, 22; Colossians 4: 12-15; 1 Thessalonians 5: 26.

It is clear that when Paul wrote letters he wrote them on the pattern which everyone used. Deissmann, the great scholar, says of the letters of Paul, " They differ from the messages of the homely papyrus leaves of Egypt, not as letters but only as the letters of Paul." When we read Paul's letters we are not reading things which were meant to be academic exercises and theological treatises, but things which are human documents written by a friend to his friends.

The Immediate Situation

With a very few exceptions all Paul's letters were written to meet an immediate situation. They are not treatises which Paul sat down to write in the peace and the silence of his study. There was some threatening situation in Corinth, or Galatia, or Philippi, or Thessalonica, and it was to meet that immediate situation that he wrote. He was not in the least thinking of us when he wrote he was thinking solely of the people to whom he was writing. Deissmann writes, " Paul had no thought of adding a few fresh compositions to the already extant Jewish epistles; still less of enriching the sacred literature of his nation. . . . He had no presentiment of the place his words would occupy in universal history; not so much that they would be in existence in the next generation, far less that one day people would look at them as Holy Scripture." We must always remember that a thing need not be a transient thing because it was written to meet an immediate situation. All the great love songs of the world were written for one person, but all the world loves them. It is just because Paul's letters were written to meet a threatening danger or a clamant need that they still throb with life. And it is because human need and the human situation do not change that God speaks to us through them to-day.

The Spoken Word

One other thing we must note about these letters of Paul. Paul did what most people did in his day. He did not normally pen his own letters; he dictated them to a secretary; and then after he had dictated them he added his own authenticating signature. We actually know the name of one of these people who did the writing for Paul. In Romans 16: 22 Tertius, the secretary, slips in his own greeting before the letter draws to an end. In I Corinthians 16: 21 Paul says, " This is my own signature, my auto-graph, so that you can be sure this letter comes from me." (cp. Colossians 4: 18; 2 Thessalonians 3: 17). This explains a great deal. Sometimes Paul is hard to understand, because his sentences begin and never finish; his grammar breaks down and his sentences become involved. We must not think of Paul sitting quietly at a desk, carefully polishing each sentence as he wrote. We must think of him striding up and down some little room, pouring out a torrent of words, while his secretary raced to get them down. When Paul composed his letters, he had in his mind's eye a vision of the folk to whom he was writing, and he was pouring out his heart to them in words that fell over each other in his eagerness to help. Paul's letters are not careful, academic products written in the seclusion of a scholar's study; they are living, vital, torrents of words poured straight from his heart to the heart of the friends for whom he wrote them.

THE LETTER TO THE GALATIANS

INTRODUCTION

Paul Under Attack

Someone has likened the letter to the Galatians to a sword flashing in a great swordsman's hand. When Paul wrote it both he and his gospel were under attack. If that attack had succeeded Christianity might have become just another Jewish sect. It might have become a thing for Jews and for Jews alone; a thing which was dependent upon circumcision and on keeping the law, instead of being a thing of grace. It is a strange thing to think that, if Paul's opponents had had their way, the gospel might have been kept for Jews, and we might never have had the chance to know the love of Christ.

Paul's Apostleship Attacked

It is impossible for a man to possess a vivid personality and a strong character like Paul and not to encounter opposition. It is impossible for a man to lead such a revolution in religious thought as Paul did and not to be attacked. The first attack was on Paul's apostleship. There were many to say that Paul was no apostle at all. From their own point of view they were right. In Acts I: 21, 22 we have the basic definition of an apostle. Judas the traitor had committed suicide; it was necessary to fill the blank made in the number of the apostolic band. How then do they define the qualifications of the man who must be chosen? He must be " one of these men who were with us during all the time our Lord went in and out amongst us, beginning from the baptism of John, until the day He was taken from us." He must be a man who was " a witness of the Resurrection." So to be an apostle a man must have companied with Jesus during His earthly

I

life, and must have witnessed the Resurrection of the Risen Lord. That qualification Paul obviously did not fulfil. Further, not only did he not fulfil that, but also, not so very long ago, he had been the arch-persecutor of the Christian Church. In the very first verse of the letter Paul answers that. Proudly he insists that the source of his apostleship is no human source and that no human hand ordained him to that office, but that he received his call direct from God. Others might have the qualifications which were demanded when the first blank in the apostolic band was filled; but Paul had a unique qualification—he had met Christ face to face on the Damascus Road.

Independence and Agreement

Further, Paul insists that for his message he was dependent on no man. That is why in chapters 1 and 2 he carefully details his visits to Jerusalem. He is insisting that he is not preaching some second-hand message which he received from a man; he is preaching a message which he received direct from Christ. But Paul was no anarchist; he was no rebel. He insisted that although his message was received in entire independence it yet had received the full approval of those who were the acknowledged leaders of the Christian Church (2: 6-10). It was Paul's insistence that the gospel he preached came direct from God to him; but that it was a gospel which was in full agreement with the faith delivered to the Church.

The Judaizers

But that gospel which Paul did preach was under attack as well. It was a struggle which had to come and a battle which had to be fought. There were Jews who had accepted Christianity; *but* they believed that all God's promises and gifts were for Jews alone and that no Gentile could be admitted to these precious privileges. They therefore believed that Christianity was for Jews and Jews alone. If Christianity was God's greatest gift to men all the more reason why none but Jews might be allowed to enjoy it. In a way that was absolutely inevitable. There was a type of Jew who arrogantly believed in the idea of the chosen people. That type of Jew could say the most terrible things—" God loves only Israel of all the nations He has made." " God will judge Israel with one measure and the Gentiles with another." " The best of the snakes crush; the best of the Gentiles kill." " God created the Gentiles to be fuel for the fires of Hell." This was the spirit which made the law lay it down that it was illegal to help a Gentile mother in her sorest hour, for that would only be to bring another Gentile into the world. Now this type of Jew saw Paul bringing the gospel to the hated and the despised Gentile and was appalled and infuriated. Because Paul preached a universal gospel they hated both him and his gospel with all their hearts.

The Law

But there was one way out of this. If a Gentile wished to become a Christian, *let him become a Jew first*. What did that mean? It meant that he must be circumcised and that he must take the whole burden of the law upon him. That, for Paul, was the very opposite of all that Christianity meant. It meant that a man's salvation was dependent on what that man could do, that it was dependent on a fleshly sign, that it was dependent on his ability to keep the law. It meant that a man by his own unaided efforts could win and earn salvation. Now, to Paul, salvation was entirely a thing of *grace*. He believed that no man could ever earn the favour of God; he believed that all that a man could do was to accept the love God offered him, to make one tremendous act of faith and fling himself, helpless, resourceless, defenceless on the love of God. The Jew would go to God saying, " Look!

3

Here are the good deeds I have done. Here is my circumcision. Here are my works. Give me the salvation I have earned." Paul would say:

> " Not the labours of my hands
> Can fulfil Thy law's demands;
> Could my zeal no respite know,
> Could my tears for ever flow,
> All for sin could not atone:
> Thou must save, and Thou alone.
>
> Nothing in my hand I bring,
> Simply to Thy Cross I cling;
> Naked, come to Thee for dress;
> Helpless, look to Thee for grace;
> Foul, I to the fountain fly;
> Wash me, Saviour, or I die."

For Paul the essential thing was, not what a man could do for God, but what God had done for him.

" But," the Jews argued, " the greatest thing in our national life is the law; and God gave that law to Moses, and on that law our very lives depend." Paul replied, " Just wait one moment. Who is the founder of our nation? To whom were the greatest of all God's promises given?" And, of course, the answer is Abraham. " Now," went on Paul, " how was it that Abraham gained the favour of God? He could not have gained it by keeping the law because he lived four hundred and thirty years before the law was given to Moses; there was no law to keep. How then did he gain it? *He gained it by an act of faith.* When God told him to leave his people and go out, Abraham trusted God so much that he made one sublime act of faith and went trusting everything to God. It was faith that saved Abraham, not law; and," says Paul, " it is faith that must save every man, not deeds of the law." " The real son of Abraham," said Paul, " is not a man who is racially descended from him and who can trace the pedigree of his body from him. The real son

4

of Abraham is the man who, no matter what his race or country or lineage, makes the same surrender of faith to God. The true Israel is not a matter of physical descent; the true Israel consists of all men who repeat Abraham's act of faith." That was Paul's argument to show that faith, and not works, brings a man within the favour of God.

The Law and Grace

If all this be true, one very serious question arises— what then is the place of the law? It cannot be denied that the law was given by God; the law is divine. Does, then, this emphasis on grace simply wipe out the law completely? The law has its own place in the scheme of things. First, the law tells men what sin is. If there is no law a man cannot break the law. If there is no law there can be no such thing as sin. The law demonstrates what sin is. And second, and most important, the law really drives a man to the grace of God. The trouble about the law is that just because we are sinful men we can never keep it perfectly. The attempt to keep it is always a losing struggle; it is a battle in which a man is always defeated. The effect of the law, therefore, is to show a man his own weakness, to drive him to a despair in which he sees that there is nothing left but to throw himself in one great act of faith on the mercy and the love of God. The law shows us our own helplessness, convinces us of our own insufficiency, and in the end compels us to admit that the only thing which can save us is not this impossible obedience to the law but the grace of God. In other words the law is an essential stage on the way to the grace of God. So, in this epistle, Paul's great theme is the glory of the grace of God, and the necessity of realizing that by our own works we can never save ourselves and that we can only surrender in utter faith to this grace of God.

5

GALATIANS

THE TRUMPET CALL OF THE GOSPEL

Galatians I: I-5

> I, Paul, an apostle—and my apostleship was given to me from no human source and through no man's hand, because it came to me direct from Jesus Christ and from God the Father, who raised Jesus from the dead—with all the brothers who are here, write this letter to the Churches of Galatia. May grace and peace be on you from God the Father and from our Lord Jesus Christ, who, because our God and Father willed it so, gave His life for our sins, to rescue us from this present world with all its evil. Glory be to Him for ever and ever. Amen.

To the people of Galatia there had come people saying that Paul was not really an apostle and that they need not listen to what he had to say. They based their belittlement of Paul on the fact that he had not been a member of the original twelve apostles, that, in fact, he had been the most savage of all persecutors of the Church, and that he held, as it were, no official appointment from the leaders of the Church. Paul's answer was not an argument; it was an unanswerable statement. He owed his apostleship to no man; he owed it to a day on the Damascus Road when he had met Jesus Christ face to face. It was Paul's claim that his office and his task had been given to him direct from God.

(i) Paul was certain that God had spoken to him. Leslie Weatherhead tells of a boy who decided to become a minister. He was asked when he had come to that decision; he replied that he had taken it after hearing a certain sermon in his school chapel. He was asked the name of the preacher who had wrought such an effect upon him. His answer was, " I do not know the preacher's name; but I know that God spoke to me that day." In the last analysis no man can make another man a minister or a servant of God. Only God can do that. The real test of a

6

Christian is not whether or not he has gone through certain ceremonies and taken certain vows; it is, has he seen Christ face to face? An old Jewish priest called Ebed-Tob said of the office which he held, " It was not my father or my mother who installed me in this place, but the arm of the Mighty King gave it to me."

(ii) The real reason for Paul's ability to toil and to suffer was that he was quite certain that his task had been given him by God. He regarded every effort that was demanded from him as a God-given task. It is not only men like Paul who have a task from God. To every man God gives his task. It may be a task of which all men will know, and which history will remember; it may be a task of which no one will ever hear; but in either case it is a task for God. Tagore has a poem like this:

> " At midnight the would-be ascetic announced:
> ' This is the time to give up my home and seek
>   for God. Ah, who has held me so long in
>   delusion here? '
> God whispered, ' I,' but the ears of the man were
>   stopped.
> With a baby asleep at her breast lay his wife,
>   peacefully sleeping on one side of the bed.
> The man said, ' Who are ye that have fooled
>   me so long? '
> The voice said again, ' They are God,' but he
>   heard it not.
> The baby cried out in its dream, nestling close
>   to its mother.
> God commanded, ' Stop, fool, leave not thy
>   home,' but still he heard not.
> God sighed and complained, ' Why does my
>   servant wander to seek me, forsaking me? ' "

There are humble tasks but they, too, are a divine apostolate. As Burns had it,

> To mak' a happy fire-side clime
> For weans and wife,
> That's the true pathos and sublime
> O' human life.

7

To Paul the God-given task was to evangelize a world; to most of us it will simply be to make one or two folk happy in the little circle of those most dear. That task, too, is of God.

Right at the beginning of his letter, Paul sums up his wishes and prayers for his friends in two tremendous words.

(i) He wishes them *grace*. There are two main ideas in the word grace. The first is the idea of *sheer beauty*. The Greek word *charis* means grace in the theological sense; but it always means beauty and charm; and even when it is theologically used the idea of charm is never far away from it. If the Christian life has grace in it it must be a lovely thing. Far too often goodness exists without charm, and charm without goodness. It is when goodness and charm unite that the work of grace is seen. The second idea is the idea of *sheer undeserved generosity*. The idea is that of a gift which a man never deserved and could never earn, and which is given to him in the generous goodness and love of the heart of God. It is a word which has in it all the love of God. When Paul prays for grace on his friends, it is as if he said, " May the beauty of the wonder of the undeserved love of God be on you, so that it will make your life lovely too."

(ii) He wishes them *peace*. Paul was a Jew, and the Jewish word *shalom* must have been in his mind, even as he wrote the Greek *eirene*. Now *shalom* means far more than the mere absence of trouble. It means everything which is to a man's highest good. It means everything which will make his mind pure, his will resolute and his heart glad. It is that sense of the love and care of God, which, even if his body were tortured, would keep a man's heart in peace and joy.

Finally, here Paul, when he speaks of Jesus, sums up in one sentence of literally infinite meaning the heart and the work of Jesus Christ. " He gave Himself . . . to rescue us." (i) The love of Christ is a love *which gave and suffered*.

8

(ii) The love of Christ is a love *which conquered and achieved*. In this life the tragedy of love is that it is so often frustrated; that it must bear the pain of loving and yet being unable to rescue the one it loves. But the love of Christ is the perfect love because it is backed by that infinite power which nothing can frustrate and which can rescue its loved one from the bondage of sin.

THE SLAVE OF CHRIST

Galatians I: 6-10

> I am amazed that you have so quickly deserted Him who called you by the grace of Christ, and that you have so soon gone over to a different gospel, a gospel which in point of fact is not another gospel at all. What has really happened is that certain men are upsetting your whole faith and are aiming at reversing the gospel of Christ. But even if we or an angel from heaven were to preach a gospel to you, other than that which you have received, let him be accursed. Is it men's favour I am trying to win, or is it God's? Or am I seeking to curry favour with men? If after all that has happened to me I were still trying to curry favour with men, I would not be bearing the brands of the slave of Christ.

THE basic fact behind the situation of this epistle is this— Paul's gospel was a gospel of free grace. He believed with all his heart that nothing a man could do could ever win the favour of God. He believed passionately that no one could ever earn the love of God. He therefore believed that all that was left for a man to do was to fling himself on the love and mercy of God in one great act of faith. He believed that all that a man could do was to take in wondering gratitude what God offers; and that the important thing was not what we could do for ourselves but what God had done for us. It was this gospel of the free grace of God that Paul had preached. After him there came men preaching a Jewish version of Christianity. They declared that, if a man wished to please God, first of all he must be circumcised; and that then he must proceed to dedicate his whole life to carrying out all the rules and regulations of the law. Every time a man performed a deed of the law, so they said, that was a credit entry in his account with God. They were teaching that it was necessary for a man to earn for himself the favour and the love of God. To Paul that was utterly impossible. Now Paul's opponents declared that Paul was making religion far too easy, and that he was doing so to curry favour with and to ingratiate himself with men. In point of fact that accusation was the reverse of the truth. After all, if religion consists in being circumcised and in fulfilling a mass of rules and regulations, it is, at least theoretically, possible to satisfy its demands. But look what Paul is saying—he is holding up the Cross and he is saying, " God loved you like that." And so religion becomes a matter, not of satisfying the claims of *law*, but of trying to meet the obligation of *love*. A man can satisfy the claims of law, for they have strict and statutory limits; but a man can never satisfy the claims of love, for if he gave his loved one the sun, the moon and the stars he still would be left feeling that that was an offering far too small. But all that Paul's Jewish opponents could see was that Paul had declared that circumcision was no longer necessary, and that the law was no longer relevant.

Paul denied that he was trying to ingratiate himself with men. It was not men he was serving; it was God. It made no difference to him what men said or thought about him; his master was God. And then he brought forward the unanswerable argument. " If," he says, " I were trying to curry favour with men I would not be the slave of Christ." What is in his mind is this—the slave was branded with his master's name and sign stamped on him with a red-hot branding iron. Paul bore on his body the marks of his campaigns, the marks of his sufferings, the brand of the slavery of Christ. " If," he said, " I were out to curry favour with men would I have these scars on me? If all I wanted was to stand well with men would I have these marks on my body?" The very fact that he was marked as he was was the final proof that his one aim was to serve Christ and not to please men.

When Paul wanted to prove that he was the servant of Christ he called his scars as his witnesses; they were his decorations, his badges of honour. John Gunther tells us of the very early communists in Russia. Many of them had been in Siberia; nearly all of them had been in prison under the Czarist régime and bore on their bodies the physical marks of what they had suffered; and he tells us that, so far from being ashamed of the marks which disfigured them, they were their greatest pride. We may be convinced that they were misguided and misguiding, but they had suffered for their cause.

It is when men see that we are prepared to suffer something for the faith which we say we hold that they will begin to believe that we really do hold it. If a thing costs us nothing men will value it at nothing.

THE ARRESTING HAND OF GOD

Galatians 1: 11-17

As for the gospel that has been preached by me, I want you to know, brothers, that it rests on no human foundation, for, neither did I receive it from any man, nor was I taught it, but it came to me through direct revelation from Jesus Christ. If you want proof of that—you heard of the kind of life I once lived when I practised the Jewish faith, a life in which I persecuted the Church of God beyond all bounds and devastated it. I was making strides in the Jewish faith beyond many of my contemporaries in my nation, for I was zealous to excess for the traditions of my fathers. It was then that God who had set me apart for a special task before I was born, and who called me through His grace, decided to reveal His Son through me, that I might tell the good news of Him amongst the Gentiles. Thereupon I did

> not confer with any human being, nor did I go up
> to Jerusalem to see those who were apostles before I
> was; but I went away to Arabia; and then I went
> back again to Damascus.

IT was Paul's contention that the gospel he preached to
men was no carried story and no second-hand tale; it
had come to him direct from God. That was a big claim
to make; a claim which demanded some kind of proof.
And for proof Paul had the courage to point to himself.
He pointed to the radical change in his own life. (i) *He
had been a fanatic for the law.* The law had been his life;
it had been the one object of his study to know it; it
had been the one effort of his life to keep it. And now the
one dominant centre of his life is *grace.* This man, who
had with passionate intensity tried to earn God's favour
and approval, was now content in humble faith to take
what God had offered. He had ceased forever to glory in
what he could do for himself; and had begun forever to
glory in what God had done for him. (ii) *He had been the
arch-persecutor of the Church.* He had devastated the
Church. The word he uses is the word for utterly sacking
a city; he had tried to make a scorched earth of the
Church; and now his one aim and object, for which he
was prepared to spend himself even to death, was to spread
that same Church over all the world. Every effect must
have an adequate cause. When a man is proceeding
headlong in one direction and suddenly turns and proceeds
headlong in precisely the opposite direction; when a man
suddenly reverses all his values so that his life turns upside
down, there must be some adequate explanation. For
Paul the explanation was the direct intervention of God.
God had laid His hand on Paul's shoulder and had arrested
him in mid-career. "That," said Paul, "is the kind of
effect which only God could produce." It is the notable
thing about Paul that he is not afraid to recount the record
of his own shame in order to show the power of God.
    He has two things to say about that intervention of God.

(i) It was no unpremeditated thing; it was in the eternal plan of God. The plan was there before ever Paul was born. A. J. Gossip tells how Alexander Whyte came to his ordination to his first charge. Whyte's message was that all through time and eternity God had been preparing this man for this congregation and this congregation for this man and, prompt to the minute, He had brought them together. Every man is an idea of God; for every man God has a plan; God sent every man into the world with a part to play in His purpose and design. It may be a big part and it may be a small part. It may be to do something of which the whole world will know, and it may be to do something of which none but the circle of those most dear will ever know. Epictetus (2: 16) says, " Have courage to look up to God and to say, ' Deal with me as Thou wilt from now on. I am as one with Thee; I am Thine; I flinch from nothing so long as Thou dost think that it is good. Lead me where Thou wilt; put on me what raiment Thou wilt. Wouldst Thou have me hold office, or eschew it, stay or fly, be rich or poor? For all this I will defend Thee before men.' " If a pagan philosopher could give himself so wholly to a God whom he knew so dimly, how much more should we!

(ii) Paul knew himself to be chosen for a task. He did not think of himself as chosen for honour, but for service; not for ease, but for battles. It is for the hardest campaigns that the general chooses his best soldiers, and for the hardest studies that the teacher chooses his best students. Paul knew that he had been saved to serve.

THE WAY OF THE CHOSEN

Galatians 1: 18-25

> Then, three years after that, I went up to Jerusalem to visit Cephas, and I stayed with him a fortnight. I saw no other apostle except James, the Lord's brother. As for what I am writing to you—before

13

God I am not lying. Then I went to the districts of Syria and Cilicia. But I remained personally unknown to the Churches of Judaea which are in Christ. The only thing they knew about me was that they were hearing the news—our one-time persecutor is preaching the faith which once he tried to devastate—and they found in me cause to glorify God.

WITH this passage we must take the last section of the passage which went before that we may see just what Paul did when the hand of God had arrested him.

(i) First, he went away to *Arabia*. He went away to be alone. He did that for two reasons. First, he had to think out this tremendous thing that had happened to him. Second, he had to speak with God before he spoke to men. He had to be sure of himself and sure of God. There are so few who will take the time to face themselves and to face God. And how can a man face the temptations, the stresses and the strains of life unless he has thought things out and thought them through, unless he is sure?

(ii) Second, he went back to *Damascus*. That was a courageous thing to do. Remember that Paul had been on the way to Damascus to wipe out the Church when God had arrested him. All Damascus knew that. Paul went back at once to bear his testimony to the people who knew best what he had been. Kipling has a famous poem called *Mulholland's Vow*. Mulholland was a cattle-man on a ship. A storm broke out and in the storm the steers broke loose. Mulholland made a bargain with God that if God saved him from these plunging horns and hooves he would serve Him from that time on. He was saved and when he got to land he proposed to keep his part of the bargain; but his idea was to preach religion where no one knew him, in comfortable circumstances, handsome and out of the wet. And then God's demand came to him, " Back you go to the cattle-boats and preach my gospel *there*." God sent him back to the place that he knew and that knew him. Our Christian witness, like our Christian charity, must begin at home.

(iii) Third, Paul went to *Jerusalem*. Again he took his life in his hands. His former friends, the Jews, would be out for his blood, because to them he was a renegade. His former victims, the Christians, might well ostracize him, unable to believe that he was a changed man. Paul had the courage to face his past. We never really get away from our past by running away from it. We can only deal with it by facing it, admitting it and defeating it.

(iv) Fourth, Paul went to *Syria and Cilicia*. It was there that Tarsus was. It was there that Paul had been brought up, that he had gone to school and learned things. There were the friends of his boyhood and his youth. Again he chose the hard way. They would no doubt regard him as quite mad; they would meet him with anger, and, worse, they would meet him with mockery. Paul was quite prepared to be regarded as a fool for the sake of Christ.

In these verses Paul is seeking to defend and prove the independence of his gospel. He got it from no man; he got it from God. He consulted no man; he consulted God. But as he wrote he unconsciously delineated himself as the man who had the courage to witness to his change and to preach his gospel in the hardest places of all.

THE MAN WHO REFUSED TO BE OVERAWED
Galatians 2: 1-10

> Fourteen years afterwards I again went up to Jerusalem with Barnabas, and I took Titus with me too. It was in consequence of a direct message from God that I went up; and I placed before them the gospel that I am accustomed to preach among the Gentiles, because I did not want to think that the work which I was trying to do, and which I had done, was going to be frustrated. This I did in private conference with those whose reputations stood high in the Church. But not even Titus, who was with me, was compelled to be circumcised, although he was a Greek. True they tried to circumcise him to please false brothers who had been furtively introduced into our society and who had insinuated themselves into our company

to spy out the liberty which we enjoy in Christ Jesus, because they wished to reduce us to their own state of servitude. Not for one hour did we yield in submission to them. We took a stand that the truth of the gospel might remain with you. Now from those who are men of reputation—what they once were makes no difference to me—there is no favouritism with God—those men of reputation imparted no fresh knowledge to me; but, on the other hand, when they saw that I had been entrusted with the preaching of the gospel in the non-Jewish world, just as Peter had been in the Jewish world—for He who worked for Peter, to make him the apostle of the Jewish world, worked for me too to make me the apostle to the non-Jewish world—and when they realized the grace that had been given to me, James, Cephas and John, whom all look upon as pillars of the Church, gave pledges of partnership to me and to Barnabas, in complete agreement that we should go to the non-Jewish world, and they to the Jewish world. The one thing which they did enjoin us to do was to remember the poor—the very thing that I myself was eager to do.

IN the preceding passage Paul has proved the independence of his gospel; he has proved that he owed it to no man, and that it had come to him direct from God. In this passage he is concerned to prove that this independence is not anarchy, and that his gospel was not something schismatic and sectarian, but was indeed no other than the faith delivered to the Church. After fourteen years' work he went up to Jerusalem, and he took with him Titus, a young friend and henchman of his, who was a Greek. That visit was by no means an easy visit. Even as he wrote there was an agitation in Paul's mind. There is a disorder in the Greek which it is not possible fully to reproduce in the English translation. It was Paul's problem that he could not say too little or he might seem to be abandoning his principles; nor could he not say too much, or it might seem that he was at open variance with the leaders of the Church. The result is that his sentences are broken and disjointed. His writing reflects the anxiety and the worry of his mind.

From the beginning the real leaders of the Church accepted his position; but there were others who were out to tame this fiery spirit. There were those, who, as we have seen, accepted Christianity, but who believed that God never gave any privilege to any man who was not a Jew; and that, therefore, before a man could become a Christian he must first be circumcised and take the whole law upon him. These Judaizers, as they are called, seized on Titus as a test case. There is a battle behind this passage; and it seems likely that the leaders of the Church urged Paul, for peace's sake, to compromise, and to give in, in the case of Titus. But Paul stood like a rock. He knew that this was a test case, and he would not yield one inch for one moment. To yield would have been to accept the slavery of the law and to turn his back on the Christian freedom which is in Christ. In the end Paul's determination won the day. In principle it was accepted that Paul's work lay in the non-Jewish world; and the work of Peter and James among the Jews. It is to be carefully noted that it is not a question of two different gospels being preached; it is a question of the same gospel being brought to two different spheres by different people specially qualified to do so.

From this picture certain characteristics of Paul are clear.

(i) Paul was a man who gave authority its due respect. He did not go his own way. He went and saw and talked with the leaders of the Church however much he might differ from them. It is a great and neglected law of life that however right we may happen to be there is nothing to be gained by rudeness. There is never any reason why courtesy and determination should not go hand in hand.

(ii) Paul was a man who refused to be overawed. Repeatedly he mentions the reputation which the leaders and pillars of the Church enjoyed. He respected them; he treated them with perfect courtesy; but he remained inflexible. There is such a thing as respect; and there is such a thing as the cringing, grovelling, prudential bowing to those whom the world or the Church labels great; but Paul was always absolutely certain that he was not seeking the approval of men, but of God.

(iii) Paul was a man conscious of a special task. He had the feeling that God had given him a task to do, and he would let neither opposition from without nor discouragement from within stop him doing it. It will always be the case that the man who knows he has a God-given task will always find that he has a God-given strength to carry it out.

THE ESSENTIAL UNITY

Galatians 2: 11-13

> But when Peter came to Antioch, I opposed him to his face because he stood condemned. Before some men arrived from James it was his habit to eat with the Gentiles. When they came he withdrew and separated himself, because he was scared of the circumcision party. The rest of the Jews played the hypocrite along with him, so that even Barnabas was led away along with them by their hypocritical actions.

THE trouble was by no means at an end. Part of the life of the early Church was a common meal; they called it the *Agape*, the Love Feast. At this feast the whole congregation came together to enjoy a common meal provided by a pooling of whatever resources they had. For many of the slaves it must have been the only decent meal they had all week; and in a very special way it marked the fellowship, the togetherness of the Christians. That seems, on the face of it, a lovely thing. But we must remember the rigid exclusiveness of the narrower Jew. The narrower Jew regarded his people as the Chosen People in such a way that it involved the rejection of all other nations. It meant for him that other nations

18

were unclean. " The Lord is merciful and gracious."
(Psalm 2: 5). " But he is only gracious to Israelites;
other nations he will terrify." " The nations are as stubble
or straw which shall be burned, or as chaff scattered to
the wind." " If a man repents God accepts him, but that
applies only to Israel and no other nation." " Love all
but hate the heretics." This exclusiveness entered into
daily life. A really strict Jew was forbidden even to do
business with a Gentile; he must not go on a journey with
a Gentile; he must neither give hospitality to, nor accept
hospitality from, a Gentile. Here, then, in Antioch arose
the tremendous problem. In face of all this could the Jews
and the Gentiles sit down together at a common meal?
If the old law and custom were to be observed it was
obviously completely impossible. Peter came to Antioch,
and, at first, he forgot the old taboos in the glory of the
new faith, and he shared the common meal with Jew and
Gentile alike. Then there came certain of the Jewish
party from Jerusalem. They used James' name but quite
certainly they were not representing James' views, and
they worked on Peter so much that Peter withdrew from
the common meal. The other Jews withdrew with him
and finally even Barnabas was involved in this secession.
It was then that Paul spoke with all the intensity of which
his passionate nature was capable. Paul saw certain
things quite clearly.

(i) A Christian Church cannot continue to be a Christian
Church if in it there are any kind of class distinctions.
The labels which men wear amongst men are irrelevant
in the presence of God. In the presence of God a man is
neither Jew nor Gentile, noble or base, rich or poor; he
is a sinner for whom Christ died. If men share in a common
sonship they must be brothers; they have a new kinship
which cuts across all earthly barriers because they are
now sons of the one Father, even God.

(ii) Paul saw that strenuous action was necessary to
counteract a drift which had occurred. He did not wait;

he struck. It made no difference to him that this drift away was connected with the name and conduct of Peter. It was wrong, and that was all that mattered to Paul. A famous name can never justify an infamous action. Paul is the vivid example of the one strong man who by his steadfastness could check a drift away from the right course before it became a tidal wave.

THE END OF THE LAW

Galatians 2: 14-17

> But when I saw that they were straying away from the right path which the gospel lays down, I said to Peter in front of them all, " If you who are a born Jew choose to live like a Gentile and not like a Jew, why are you forcing the Gentiles to live like Jews? We are by nature Jews; we are not Gentile sinners as you would call them; and we know that a man is not put right with God because he does the works which the law lays down, but through faith in Jesus Christ. Now we have accepted this faith in Jesus Christ, so that we might be right with God, and that faith has nothing to do with the works the law lays down, because no man can ever put himself right with God by doing the works the law lays down. Now if in our search to be made right with God through Christ Jesus we too become what you call sinners, are you then going to argue that Christ is the minister of sin? God forbid! "

HERE at last the real root of the matter is being reached. A decision is being forced which could not in any event be long delayed. The fact of the matter was that the Jerusalem decision was a compromise, and, like all compromises, it had in it the seeds of trouble. In effect the Jerusalem decision was that the Jews would go on living like Jews, observing circumcision and the law, but that the Gentiles were free from these observances. Clearly, things could not go on like that, because the inevitable result was to produce two grades of Christians and two quite distinct classes in the Church. Paul's argument runs like this. He said to Peter, " You shared the table with the Gentiles; you ate and lived as they ate; therefore you approved in principle that there is one way for Jew and Gentile alike. How can you now reverse your whole decision? You were quite willing to live like a Gentile; and now you have swung round, and you want the Gentiles to be circumcised and take the law upon them and become Jews." The thing did not make sense to Paul. And now we must make sure of the meaning of one word. When the Jew used the word *sinners* of Gentiles he was not thinking of moral qualities at all; he was thinking of the observance of the law. To take an example—Leviticus 11 lays down the Jewish food laws and enumerates and classifies the animals which they may and may not use for food. A man who ate a hare, or who ate pork, broke those laws and became a *sinner* in this sense of the term. So Peter would answer Paul, " But, if I eat with the Gentiles and eat the things they eat, I become a sinner." Paul's answer is twofold. First, he says, " We have agreed long ago that no amount of observance of the law can make a man right with God. That is a matter of grace. A man cannot earn, he must accept, the generous offer of the love of God. It is utter trust in the love of God in Jesus that puts a man right with God. Therefore the whole business of law is irrelevant anyhow." Then he uses another argument to drive his opponent into a corner from which there is no escape. " You hold," he says, " that to forget all this business about laws and rules and regulations will make you a sinner. *But that is precisely what Jesus Christ told you to do.* He did not tell you to try to earn salvation by eating this animal and not eating that one. He told you to fling yourself without reserve on the grace of God. Are you going to argue, then, that Jesus Christ taught you to become a sinner?" Obviously there is only one answer to that; and the answer means that the old laws are simply wiped out.

This is the point that had to come. It could not be right for Gentiles to come to God by grace and Jews to come to God by law. For Paul there was only one reality, and that was grace, and by the way of surrender to that grace all men must come.

There are two great temptations in the Christian life, and, in a certain sense, the better a man is the more liable he is to them. First, there is the temptation to try to earn the favour of God, and to God man can never give; from God he must always take. Second, there is the temptation that the man who has some little achievement to show will compare himself with his fellow men to his advantage and to their disadvantage. The Christianity which has enough of self left in it to think that by its own efforts it can please God and that by its own achievements it can show itself superior to the normal run of men, is not true Christianity at all.

THE LIFE THAT IS CRUCIFIED AND RISEN

Galatians 2: 18-21

> If I build up again these very things that I destroyed, I simply succeed in making myself a transgressor. For through the law I died to the law that I might live to God. I have been crucified with Christ. True, I am alive; but it is no longer I who live but Christ who lives in me. The life that I am now living, although it is still in the flesh, is a life which is lived in faith in the Son of God, who loved me and gave Himself for me. I am not going to cancel out the grace of God; for if I can get right with God by means of the law, then Christ died quite unnecessarily.

HERE Paul speaks out of the depths of personal experience. For him to re-erect the whole fabric of the law would have been spiritual suicide. He says that through the law he died to the law that he might live to God. What he means is this—he had tried the way of law; he had tried with all the terrible intensity of his hot heart to win God's favour, to put himself right with God, by a life that sought to obey every single item of the law. He had found that such an attempt left him with nothing but a deeper and deeper sense of failure, and nothing but a deeper and deeper sense that all he could do could never put him right with God. All that the law had done was to show him his own helplessness. Whereupon he had quite suddenly abandoned the whole way of law and had cast himself, sinner as he was, on the mercy of God. It was the law which had driven him to God. To go back to the law would simply have entangled him all over again in that deadly miasma of the sense of estrangement from God. So great was that change that the only way he could describe it was to say that he had been crucified with Christ and the man he used to be was dead. And now the living power within him was nothing other than Christ Himself. " If I can put myself to rights with God by meticulously obeying the law then what is the need of grace? If I can win my own salvation then why had Christ to die? "

Paul was quite sure of one thing—that Jesus Christ had done for him what he could never have done for himself. The one man who re-enacted the experience of Paul was Martin Luther. Luther was a show-piece of discipline and penance, and self-denial and self-torture. " If ever," he said, " a man could be saved by monkery that man was I." He had gone to Rome; it was considered to be an act of great merit to climb the Scala Sancta, the great sacred stairway, on hands and knees. He toiled upwards seeking that merit that he might win; and suddenly there came to him the voice from heaven, " The just shall live by faith." The life at peace with God was not to be attained by this futile, never-ending, ever-defeated effort; it could only be had by casting himself on the love and mercy of God as Jesus Christ revealed them to men. It is when a man gives up the struggle which the pride of self thinks it can win, but must ever lose,

and when he abandons himself to the forgiving love of
God that peace must come.

> " Pining souls! come nearer Jesus,
>   And O come, not doubting thus,
> But with faith that trusts more bravely
>   His huge tenderness for us.

> If our love were but more simple,
>   We should take Him at His word;
> And our lives would be all sunshine,
>   In the sweetness of our Lord."

When Paul took God at His word the midnight of law's
frustration became the sunshine of grace.

THE GIFT OF GRACE

Galatians 3: 1-9

O senseless Galatians, who has put the evil eye on
you—you before whose very eyes Jesus Christ was
placarded upon His Cross? Tell me this one thing—
did you receive the Spirit by doing the works the
law lays down, or because you listened and believed?
Are you so senseless? After beginning your experience
of God in the Spirit, are you now going to try to
complete it by making it dependent upon what human
nature can do? Is the tremendous experience you
had all for nothing—if indeed you are going to let
it go for nothing? Did He who generously gave you
the Spirit, and who wrought mighty things among
you, do so because you produced the deeds the law
lays down or because you heard and believed? Was it
not with you exactly as it was with Abraham—
Abraham trusted God, and it was that which was
credited to him as righteousness. So you must realize
that it is those who make the venture of faith who
are the sons of Abraham. Scripture foresaw that it
would be by faith that God would bring the Gentiles
into a right relationship with Himself, and told the
good news to Abraham before it happened—In you
shall all nations be blessed. So, then, it is those who
make that same venture of faith who are blessed
along with Abraham, the man of faith.

HERE Paul uses still another argument to show that it is trust in God and not works of the law which puts a man right with God. In the early Church converts nearly always received the Holy Spirit in a perfectly visible and manifest way. The early chapters of Acts show that happening again and again. (cp. Acts 8: 14-17; 10: 44). There came to them a new surge of life and power that anyone could see. That experience had happened to the Galatians. It had happened, said Paul unanswerably, not because they had obeyed the regulations of the law, because at that time they had never heard of the law, but because they had heard the good news of the love of God and had responded to it in an act of perfect trust.

Now the easiest way to grasp an idea is to see that idea embodied in a person. In a sense, every great word must become flesh. So Paul pointed the Galatians to a man who embodied faith. That man was Abraham. Abraham was the man to whom God had made the great promise that in him all families of the earth would be blessed. (Genesis 12: 3). He was the man whom God had specially chosen as the man who pleased Him. Wherein did Abraham specially please God? It was not by doing the works of the law, because at that time the law did not exist; it was by taking God at His word, by trusting God entirely, by abandoning all earthly things and surrendering himself in one great act of faith. Now the promise of blessedness was made to the descendants of Abraham. On that the Jew relied; he held that simple physical descent from Abraham set him on a different footing with God from other men. Paul changes all that. He declares that to be a descendant of Abraham is not a matter of flesh and blood descent; the real descendant of Abraham is the man who in every day and generation makes the same act and venture of faith. Therefore, it is not those who seek merit through the law who inherit the promise made to Abraham; but those who, in every nation, repeat Abraham's act of faith in God. It was by an act of faith that the Galatians had begun. Surely, demands Paul, they are not going to slip back into legalism—and lose their inheritance.

This passage is uniquely full of Greek words with a history, words which carried an atmosphere and a story with them. In verse I Paul speaks about *the evil eye*. The Greeks had a great fear of a spell cast by the evil eye. Time and again private letters end with some such sentence as this: " Above all I pray that you may be in health *unharmed by the evil eye* and faring prosperously." (Milligan, *Selections from the Greek Papyri*, No. I4). In the same verse he talks about Jesus Christ being *placarded* before them upon His Cross. It is the Greek word (*prographein*) that would be used for putting up a poster. It is actually used for a notice put up by a father to say that he will no longer be responsible for his son's debts; it is also used for putting up the announcement of an auction sale. In verse 4 Paul talks about *beginning* their experience in the Spirit and *ending* it in the flesh. The words Paul uses are the words which are the normal Greek words for beginning and completing a sacrifice. The first one (*enarchesthai*) is the word for scattering the grains of barley on and around the victim which was the first act of a sacrifice; and the second one (*epiteleisthai*) is the word used for fully completing the ritual of any sacrifice. By using these two words Paul shows that he looks on the whole Christian life as a sacrifice to God. In verse 5 he speaks of God giving generously to the Galatians. The root of this word is the Greek word *choregia*. In the ancient days in Greece at the great festivals the great dramatists like Euripides and Sophocles presented their plays; Greek plays all have a chorus; to equip and train a chorus was expensive, and public-spirited Greeks generously offered to defray the entire expenses of the chorus; later, in war time, patriotic citizens gave free contributions to the state. That is described by the word *choregia*. In still later Greek, in the papyri, the word is common in marriage contracts and describes the support that a husband, out of his love, undertakes to give his wife. The word underlines the generosity of God, a generosity which is born of love, of which the love of the citizen for his city and of a man for his wife are dim suggestions.

THE CURSE OF THE LAW

Galatians 3: 10-14

> All who depend on the deeds which the law lays down are under a curse, for it stands written, " Cursed is everyone who does not consistently obey and perform all the things written in the book of the law." It is clear that no one ever gets into a right relationship with God by means of this legalism, because, as the Bible says, " It is the man who is right with God through faith who will live." But the law is not based on faith. And yet the scripture says, " The man who does these things will have to live by them." Christ ransomed us from the curse of the law by becoming accursed for us—for it stands written, " Cursed is every man who is hanged on a tree." And this all happened so that in Christ Abraham's blessing should come to the Gentiles, and so that we might receive the promised Spirit by means of faith.

HERE again Paul's argument seeks to drive his opponents into a corner from which there is no escape. " Suppose," he says, " you do decide that you are going to take the course of trying to win God's favour and approval by means of accepting and obeying the law, suppose you do try to get into a right relationship with God that way, what, then, is the logical and inevitable consequence? " First of all, the man who does that has to stand or fall by his decision; if he chooses the law he has got to live by the law. Second, it is impossible to do it; no man ever has, and no man ever will, succeed in always keeping and obeying and satisfying the law. Third, if that is so then you are accursed, because scripture itself says (Deuteronomy 27: 26) that the man who does not keep the whole law is under a curse. Therefore, the logical and inevitable end of trying to get right with God by making law the principle of life is a curse. But scripture has another saying, " It is the man who is right with God by faith who will really live." (Habakkuk 2: 4). So, then, the only way to get into a right relationship with God, and therefore the only way to peace, is the way of faith, of acceptance, of surrender. But the principle of law and the principle of faith are quite antithetic; you cannot direct your life by both at one and the same time; you must choose; and therefore the only logical choice is to abandon the way of legalism and to venture upon the way of faith, of taking God at His word and of trusting His love.

And how can we know that all this is so? The final guarantor of its truth is Jesus Christ; and to bring this truth to us Christ had to die upon His Cross. Now, scripture says that every man who is hanged on a tree is accursed (Deuteronomy 21: 23); and so to free us of the curse of the law Jesus Himself had to become accursed. Jesus had to become accursed to tell us of the love of God.

Even at his most involved, and here he is involved, one simple yet tremendous fact is never far from the mind and the heart of Paul—*the cost of the Christian gospel*. He could never forget that the peace, the liberty, the right relationship with God that we possess cost the life and death of Jesus Christ, for how could men ever have known what God was like unless Jesus Christ had died to tell them that He loves them like that?

THE COVENANT THAT CANNOT BE ALTERED

Galatians 3: 15-18

> Brothers, I can but use only a human analogy. Here is the parallel—when a covenant is duly ratified, even if it is only a man's covenant, no one annuls it or adds additional clauses to it. Now the promises

LETTERS TO THE GALATIANS AND EPHESIANS

were made to Abraham and to his *seed*. It does not
say, " and to his *seeds*," as if it were a case of *many*,
but, " and to his *seed*," as if it were a case of *one*,
and that one is Christ. This is what I mean, the
law which came into being four hundred and thirty
years later cannot annul the covenant already ratified
by God and thus render the promise inoperative.
For, if the inheritance is dependent on law, it is no
longer dependent on promise; but it was through
promise that God conferred his grace on Abraham.

WHEN we read a passage like this and like the next one
we have always to remember that Paul was a trained
Rabbi; he was an expert in the scholastic methods of
the Rabbinic academies. He could, and did, use their
methods of argument, which would be completely cogent
and convincing to a Jew, however difficult they may be
for us to follow and to understand. Paul's aim is to show
the superiority of the way of grace over the way of law.
He begins by showing that the way of grace is older than
the way of law. When Abraham had made his venture
of faith, God had made his great promise to Him. That
is to say, God's promise had been made consequent upon
an act of faith; the basis of the covenant between God
and Abraham was faith. Now the law did not come until
the time of Moses, and that was four hundred and thirty
years later. But—Paul goes on to argue—once a covenant,
an agreement, a will, has been duly agreed and ratified,
you cannot alter it, and you cannot add additional clauses
and codicils to it; it must remain unchanged. Therefore,
the later law cannot alter the earlier way of faith. It
was faith which set Abraham right with God; the law
can never alter that; and faith is still the only way for a
man to get himself right with God.

The Rabbis were very fond of using arguments which
depend on the meaning and the use and the interpretation
of single words. They would erect a whole theology on
a single word. Now Paul takes one single word in the
Abraham story and erects an argument upon it. Paul

goes back to the old promise to Abraham as we find it in Genesis 17: 7, 8. There God says to Abraham, " I will establish my covenant between me and thee and thy *seed* after thee." God says of Abraham's inheritance, " I will give it unto thee and to thy *seed* after thee." To make it clear, let us substitute one word for the word *seed*. Instead of seed let us say *descendant*. Paul's argument is that the word *seed* is used in the *singular* and not in the *plural*; and that, therefore, God's promise points not to a great crowd of people but to *one single individual*; and—argues Paul—the one person in which the covenant finds its consummation is Jesus Christ. And, therefore, the way to peace and right relations with God is the way of faith which Abraham took, the way in which God's promise came to him; and we must repeat that way by looking to Jesus Christ with perfect faith.

Again and again Paul comes back to the same point. The whole problem of human life is to get into a right relationship with God. So long as we are afraid of God, so long as God is a grim stranger, there can be no peace in life. How can we achieve this right relationship? Shall we try to achieve it by a meticulous and even self-torturing obedience to the law, by performing endless deeds, by observing every smallest regulation the law lays down? If we take that way we are forever in default, for man's imperfection can never fully satisfy the perfection of God; we are forever frustrated, forever climbing up a hill in which the peak never comes in sight, forever under condemnation; but if we simply abandon this hopeless struggle and bring ourselves and our sin to God, then the grace of God opens its arms to us and we are at peace with a God who is no longer judge but father. Paul's whole argument is that that is what happened to Abraham; it was on that basis that God's covenant with Abraham was made. And nothing that came in later can change that covenant any more than anything can alter a will that has already been ratified and signed.

SHUT UP UNDER SIN

Galatians 3: 19-22

> Why, then, have the law at all? The law was added
> to the situation to define what transgressions are,
> until the seed should come, to whom the promise,
> which still holds good, had been made. That law
> was enacted by angels and came by means of a mediator.
> Now there can be no such thing as a mediator of
> one; and God is one. Is, then, the law contrary
> to the promises of God? God forbid! If a law which
> was able to give life had been given, then indeed right
> relationship with God would have come through
> the law. But the words of scripture shut up everything
> under the power of sin, for the very reason that the
> promise should be given to those who believe through
> faith in Jesus Christ.

THIS is one of the most difficult passages that Paul ever
wrote. So difficult is it that there are almost three hundred
different interpretations of it! Let us begin by remembering
that Paul is still seeking to demonstrate the superiority
of the way of grace and faith over the way of law. He
makes three points about the law. (i) Why introduce
the law at all? It was introduced, as Paul puts it, *for the
sake of transgressions*. What he means is this—it is a
favourite thought of Paul that where there is no law there
is no sin. You cannot break a law that does not exist.
Before a man can be branded as a sinner he must know
the law. He cannot be condemned for doing a wrong
thing if he did not know that it was the wrong thing.
Therefore the function of the law is *to define sin*. But,
while the law can and does define sin, it can do nothing
whatever to cure sin. There is at one and the same time
the strength and the weakness of the law. The strength
of the law is that it defines sin; its weakness is that it
can do nothing to cure sin. It is alike a doctor who is an
expert in diagnosis but who is helpless to clear up the
trouble which he has diagnosed. (ii) The law was not
given direct by God. In the old story in Exodus 20 the
law was given direct to Moses; but in the days of Paul

the Rabbis were so impressed by the utter holiness and the utter distance and remoteness of God that they believed that it was quite impossible for God to deal direct with men; therefore they introduced the idea that the law was given first to angels and then by the angels to Moses. (cp. Acts 7: 53; Hebrews 2: 2). Here Paul is using the Rabbinic thoughts of his time. The law then is at a double remove from God. It was given first to angels; and then to a mediator, and the mediator is Moses. Compared with the *promise*, which was given absolutely directly by God, the *law* is a second-hand thing which came through intermediaries. (iii) Now we come to that extraordinarily difficult sentence—" There can be no such thing as a mediator of one; and God is one." What is Paul's thought here? An agreement founded on law always involves *two* people. There is the person who gives it and the person who accepts it. That agreement is dependent on the action of *two* people. Let the one who receives the conditions break them and the whole agreement collapses. Any legal agreement depends on both sides keeping the agreement. That is the position those who put their trust in the law were in. Break that law, and the whole agreement is undone. But a promise only depends on *one* person; the promise is given by one, and nothing anyone else can do can break or alter that promise. Now the way of grace depends entirely on God; it is His promise, His grace, His love. Nothing man can do can alter that. He may sin, he may stray, but the love and the grace of God stand unaltered. To Paul it was the weakness of the law that it depended on *two* persons; it depended not only on the law-giver; it depended on man's keeping it. And man had wrecked it. But grace is entirely of God; nothing man can do can undo it; and surely, beyond all argument, it is better to depend on the grace of the unchanging God than on the doomed to failure efforts of helpless men. (iv) Is, then, the law quite antithetic to grace? Logically Paul should answer, " Yes," in fact, he answers, " No."

He says that scripture has shut up everyone under sin. He is thinking of Deuteronomy 27: 26 where it is said that everyone who does not conform to the words of the law is cursed. Now, in point of fact, that means *everyone*, because no one ever has, or ever will, perfectly keep the law. What, then, is the consequence of the law? The consequence of the law is simply to drive everyone to seek grace, because it has proved man's helplessness. This is a thought that Paul will soon develop in the next chapter. Here he only suggests it and hints at it. The great value of the law, the supreme place of the law, was to drive a man to grace when he found how helpless he was to satisfy it. Let a man try to get into a right relationship with God via the law; he will find he cannot do it, and he will be driven to see that all he can do is to accept the wonder of grace of which Jesus Christ came to tell men.

THE COMING OF FAITH

Galatians 3: 23-29

> Before faith came we were under guard under the power of the law, shut up and waiting for the day when faith would be revealed. So that the law was really our tutor to bring us to Christ so that we might get into a right relationship with God by means of faith. But now that faith has come we are no longer under a tutor; for you are all sons of God through faith in Christ Jesus. As many of you as have been baptized into Christ have put on Christ. There is no longer any distinction between Jew and Greek, slave and free man, male and female, for you are all one in Christ Jesus. And if you belong to Christ, then you are the seed of Abraham, and heirs according to promise.

In this passage Paul is still thinking of the essential part that the law did play in the plan and economy of God. In the Greek world there was a household servant called the *paidagogos*. He was not the schoolmaster. He was

33

usually an old and trusted slave who had been long in the family and whose character was high. He was in charge of the child's moral welfare. It was his duty to see that the child ran into no temptation or danger and that he acquired the qualities essential to true manhood. He had one particular duty; every day he had to take the child to and from school. He had nothing to do with the actual teaching of the child, but it was his duty to take him in safety to the school and to deliver him to the teacher. That—said Paul—was like the function of the law. The law was there to lead a man to Christ; it could not take him into Christ's presence; but it could take him into a position where the man himself might enter. It was the function of the law to bring a man to Christ by showing him that by himself he was utterly unable to keep the law. That very sense of failure and of inadequacy led a man to Christ. But once a man had come to Christ he no longer needed the law, for now he was dependent not on law but on grace.

" As many of you," says Paul, " who have been baptized into Christ have put on Christ." There are two vivid pictures here. Baptism was a Jewish rite and custom. If a man wished to accept the Jewish faith he had to do three things. He had to be circumcised, to offer sacrifice and to be baptized. Ceremonial washing to cleanse from defilement was very common in Jewish practice. (cp. Leviticus, chapters 11 to 15). The details of Jewish baptism were as follows:—The man to be baptized cut his hair and his nails; he undressed completely; the baptismal bath must contain 40 seahs, that is 2 hogsheads, of water. Every part of the body had to be touched with the water. He made confession of his faith before three men who were called *fathers of baptism*. While still in the water parts of the law were read to him, words of encouragement were addressed to him, and benedictions were pronounced upon him. When he emerged he was a member of the Jewish faith. It was through baptism that he entered

34

into the Jewish faith; he was baptized into that faith.
By Christian baptism a man entered into Christ. The early
Christians looked on baptism as something which really
and truly produced a real union with Christ. It is of course
to be noted that in a missionary situation, where men
were coming direct from heathenism, baptism was for
the most part adult baptism, and the adult would
necessarily have an experience a child could not have.
But just as really as the Jewish convert was united with
and received into the Jewish faith, the Christian convert
was united with and entered into Christ. (cp. Romans
6: 3ff; Colossians 2: 12). Baptism was no mere outward
form and ceremony; it was a real union with Christ. Paul
goes on to say that they had put on Christ. There may
be here a reference to a custom which certainly existed
later. The candidate for baptism was clothed in pure white
robes, symbolic of the new life into which he had entered.
Just as the initiate put on his new white robe he put on
Christ; his life was clothed with Christ.

The result of all this is that in the Church there is no
difference between any of the members; they have all
become sons of God. In verse 28 Paul says that the dis-
tinction between Jew and Greek, slave and free man,
male and female is wiped out. There is something of very
great interest here. In the Jewish form of morning prayer,
which Paul must all his pre-Christian life have used,
there is a thanksgiving in which the Jew thanks God that
" Thou hast not made me a Gentile, a slave or a woman."
Paul takes that prayer and reverses it. The old distinctions
are gone; for the disunity there is unity; for the separation
there is communion; all are one in Christ.

Now we have already seen (verse 16) that Paul interprets
the promises made to Abraham as specially finding their
fulfilment in Christ; and if we are one with Christ then
we too inherit the promises—and this great privilege
came to us not by a legalistic keeping of the law, but
by act of faith in the generous and free grace of God.

There is only one thing which can wipe out the ever sharpening distinctions and differences and separations between man and man. When all are debtors to God's grace, and when all are in Christ, then and only then all will be one. It is not the force of man but the love of God which alone can unite a disunited world.

THE DAYS OF CHILDHOOD

Galatians 4: 1-7

> This is what I mean—so long as the heir is an infant there is no difference between him and a slave, although he is owner of everything, but he is under the control of stewards and overseers until the day which his father has fixed arrives. It is just the same with us. When we were infants we were in subjection to the elementary knowledge which this world can supply. But when the fulness of time came, God sent forth His Son, born of a woman, born under the law, in order that He might redeem those who were subject to the law, so that we might be adopted as sons. Because you are sons, God sent forth the Spirit of His Son into our hearts, crying " Abba! Father! " The consequence is that you are no longer a slave but a son; and if a son, an heir because God made you so.

IN the ancient world the process of growing up was much more definite than it is with us. (i) In the Jewish world, when a boy had passed his twelfth birthday, on the first Sabbath after it, the father took the boy to the Synagogue, where he became *A Son of the Law*. The father thereupon uttered a benediction, " Blessed be Thou, O God, who has taken from me the responsibility for this boy." The boy prayed a prayer in which he said, " O my God and God of my fathers! On this solemn and sacred day, which marks my passage from boyhood to manhood, I humbly raise my eyes unto Thee, and declare with sincerity and truth, that henceforth I will keep Thy commandments, and undertake and bear the responsibility of mine actions towards Thee." There was a clear dividing line in the boy's life. Almost overnight the boy became a man. (ii) In Greece the boy was under his father's care from seven until he was eighteen. He then became what was called an *ephebos*, which may be translated *cadet*, and for two years he was under the direction of the state. The Athenians were divided into ten *phratriai*, or *clans*. Before a lad became an *ephebos*, at a festival called the *Apatouria*, he was received into the clan; and at a ceremonial act his long hair was cut off and offered to the gods. Once again, growing up was a quite definite process. (iii) Under Roman law the year at which a boy grew up was not definitely fixed, but it was always between the ages of fourteen and seventeen. At a sacred festival in the family called the *Liberalia* he took off the *toga prætexta*, which was a toga with a narrow purple band at the foot of it and put on the *toga virilis*, which was a plain toga which adults wore. He was then conducted by his friends and relations down to the forum and formally introduced to public life. It was essentially a religious ceremony. And once again there was a quite definite day on which the lad grew up. There was a Roman custom that on the day a boy or girl grew up, the boy offered his ball, and the girl her doll, to Apollo to show that he or she had put away childish things. When a boy was an *infant* in the eyes of the law he might be in reality the owner of a vast property, but he could take no legal decision; he was not in control of his own life; everything was done and directed for him; and, therefore, for all practical purposes he had no more freedom than if he were a slave; but when he became a man he entered into his full inheritance and into the liberty of manhood.

So—Paul argues—in the childhood of the world, the law held sway. But the law was only elementary knowledge. To describe it Paul uses the word *stoicheia*. A *stoicheion* was originally a line of things, for instance, it can mean a file of soldiers. But it came to mean the A B C; and then to mean any elementary teaching or knowledge. We must note that it has still another meaning which some would see here. It can also mean the elements of which the world is composed, and in particular, the stars. Now the ancient world was haunted by a belief in astrology. If a man was born under a certain star his fate, they believed, was fixed and settled. Men lived under the tyranny of the stars and longed for the secret release. Some scholars think that Paul is here saying that, at one time, the Galatians had been haunted and terrified and tyrannised by their belief in the baleful influence of the stars. But the whole passage seems to make it necessary to take *stoicheia* in the sense of elementary, rudimentary knowledge. So Paul says, when the Galatians—and indeed all men— were mere helpless children, they were under the tyranny of the law; then, when everything was ready, came Christ, and Christ released men from the tyranny of the law. So now men are no longer slaves of the law; they have become sons and have entered into their inheritance. The childhood which belonged to the law should be past; the freedom of manhood has come.

The proof that we are sons comes from the instinctive cry of the heart. In man's deepest need, man looks up and cries, " Father! " to God. Paul uses the double phrase, " Abba! Father! " *Abba* is the Aramaic word for Father. It must have been often on Jesus' lips, and the sound of it was so sacred that men kept it in the original tongue. This instinctive cry of the heart of man, Paul believes to be the work of the Holy Spirit; and if our hearts so cry then we know that we are sons, and all the inheritance of grace is ours. For Paul, the man who governed his life by slavery to the law was still a child; the man who had learned the way of grace had become a mature, full-grown man in the Christian faith.

38

PROGRESS IN REVERSE

Galatians 4: 8-11

> There was a time when you did not know God, and when you were slaves to gods who are no gods at all; but now that you know God—or rather now that God knows you—how can you turn back again to the weak and poverty-stricken elementary things, for it is to them that you wish to be enslaved all over again? You meticulously observe days and months and seasons and years. I am afraid for you, lest all the labour I spent on you is to go for nothing.

IN this passage Paul is still basing his thought on the conception that the law is an elementary stage in religion, and that the mature man is the man who takes his stand on grace. The law was all right in the old days when they did not know any better. But now they have come to know God and the grace of God. And then Paul corrects himself—man cannot by his own efforts know God; God of His grace reveals Himself to man. We can never seek God unless He has already found us. So now Paul demands, " Are you now going to go back to a stage that you should have left behind long ago? Are you going to make progress in reverse? "

Paul calls the elementary things, the religion based on law, *weak and poverty-stricken*. (i) It is *weak* because it is helpless. It can define sin; it can show a man when he is sinning; it can convict him of sin; but it can neither find for him forgiveness for past sin nor strength to conquer future sin. The law's basic and inherent weakness always was, and is, that it can diagnose the disease but it cannot produce a cure. (ii) It is *poverty-stricken* in comparison with the splendour of grace. In its very nature the law can only deal with one situation. For every fresh situation man needs a fresh law; but the wonder of grace was that it is *poikilos*, which means *variegated, many-coloured*. That is to say, there is not a possible situation in life which grace cannot match. The law, as it were, goes stumbling from crisis to crisis; grace is sufficient for all things.

One of the features of Jewish law was its observance of special days and seasons. In this passage the *days* are the Sabbaths of each week; the *months* are the new moons which were special occasions; the *seasons* are the great annual feasts like the Passover, Pentecost and the Feast of Tabernacles; the *years* are the Sabbatic years, every seventh year, which was a special year. The failure of a religion which is dependent on special days and seasons is that almost inevitably it divides days into sacred and secular, days which belong to God and days with which men can do as they like; and the further almost inevitable step is that when a man has meticulously observed the special days he is very liable to think that he has discharged his duty to God. Although that was the religion of legalism it was very far from being the prophetic religion. It has been said that, " The ancient Hebrew people had no word in their language to correspond to the word ' religion ' as it is commonly used to-day. The whole of life as they saw it came from God, and was subject to His law and governance. There could be no separate part of it in their thought labelled ' religion.' Jesus Christ did not say, ' I am come that ye may have religion,' but, ' I am come that ye might have life, and that ye might have it more abundantly.' " To make religion a thing of days and times and seasons is to make it entirely an external thing. For the real Christian every day is God's day. It was Paul's fear that men who had once known the splendour of grace would slip back to legalism, and that men who had once lived in the presence of God would shut God up to special days.

LOVE'S APPEAL

Galatians 4: 12-20

> Brothers, I entreat you, become as I am, because I became as you are. I have no complaints against the way that once you treated me. You know that

it was because I was ill that I first preached the gospel to you. It must have been a temptation to you to do so, but you did not look on me with contempt or turn with loathing from me, but you received me as if I were an angel of God, as you would have received Christ Jesus. I once had cause to congratulate you. Where has that cause gone to? I am prepared to give evidence in your favour that you would have dug out your eyes and given them to me. So then—have I become your enemy because I tell you the truth? It is not for any honourable reason that these other people pay court to you, but because they wish to put the barriers up so that you will have to pay court to them. It is always a fine thing to be zealous in a fine affair, and that not only when I am actually present with you. My little children, for whom I suffer the birth-pangs all over again, until you have taken the form of Christ, I wish I could be with you now! I wish that I had not to talk like this to you, because I am worried about you.

HERE Paul makes, not a theological, but a personal appeal; here he is using not the argument of the intellect but the appeal of the heart. He reminds them that for their sake he had become a Gentile; he had abandoned the ways and privileges of his people; he had cut adrift from the traditions in which he had been brought up; he had become what they are; and now his appeal is that they should not seek to become Jews, but that they might become like himself.

Here we have a reference to Paul's thorn in the flesh. It was through illness that first they met him, and that first he came to them. We shall discuss the thorn more fully when we come to the classic passage in 2 Corinthians 12: 7. It has been held to be the persecution which he suffered; the temptations of the flesh which he is said never to have succeeded in suppressing; his physical appearance which the Corinthians regarded as contemptible. (2 Corinthians 10: 10). The oldest tradition is that the thorn refers to violent and prostrating headaches. From this passage itself there emerge two indications. The

Galatians would have given him their eyes if they could have done so. It has been suggested that Paul's eyes forever troubled him, because he had been dazzled so much by the glory of the Damascus Road that ever afterwards he could see but dimly and painfully. The word that is translated *you did not turn from me with loathing* literally means *you did not spit at me*. Now in the ancient world it was the custom for a man to spit when he met an epileptic to avert the influence of the evil spirit which they believed to be resident in the sufferer; so it has been suggested that Paul was an epileptic. Let us see if we can find out just when Paul came to Galatia and it may be possible to deduce why he came. It is very possible that Acts 13: 13, 14 describe Paul's coming to Galatia. That passage presents a problem. Paul and Barnabas and Mark had come from Cyprus to the mainland. They came to Perga in Pamphylia; there Mark left them; and then they proceeded straight to Antioch in Pisidia, which is in the province of Galatia. Why did Paul not preach in Pamphylia? It was a populous district. Why did he choose to go to Antioch in Pisidia? The road that led there, up into the central plateau, was one of the most difficult and dangerous roads in the world. That is probably why Mark left and went home. Why this sudden flight from Pamphylia? The reason may well be this—Pamphylia and the coastal plain were districts where malarial fever raged; it is more than probable that Paul contracted this malaria, and his only remedy was to seek the highlands of Galatia; and that, therefore, he arrived amongst the Galatians a sick man. Now this malaria recurs and it is accompanied by a prostrating headache which those who have experienced it liken to " a red-hot bar thrust through the forehead," or a dentist's drill boring through the temple. It may well have been that it was this terrible, incurable, prostrating pain which was Paul's thorn in the flesh, and which was torturing him when first he came to Galatia.

He talks about those who were sedulously paying court

to the Galatians; he means those who were seeking to
persuade them to adopt Jewish ways. They were only
courting them to put the barriers up. If they could persuade
the Galatians to adopt Jewish ways then the Galatians
would have to pay humble court to them to be allowed
to be circumcised and to enter the Jewish nation. These
people paid court to the Galatians, but they only did so
to get control of them and to reduce them to subjection
to themselves and to the law.

In the end Paul uses a vivid metaphor. His bringing
the Galatians to Christ cost him a pain like a mother's
travail; and now he has to go through it all again. Christ
is in them, as it were in embryo. He has to bring them to
birth in Christ.

No one can fail to see the deep affection of the last
words. *My little children*—diminutives in Latin and Greek
always express deep affection. John often uses this expression, but Paul uses it nowhere else; his heart is running
over. We do well to note that Paul did not scold with
bitter words. He yearned over his straying children. It
was said of Florence Allshorn, the famous missionary
and teacher, that if she had cause to rebuke any of her
students she did so, as it were, with her arm around them.
The accent of love will penetrate where the tones of anger
will never find a way.

AN OLD STORY AND A NEW MEANING

Galatians 4: 21—5: 1

> Tell me this—you who want to be subject to the law,
> you listen to it being read to you, don't you? Well,
> then, it stands written in it that Abraham had two
> sons; one was the son of the slave girl, and one was
> the son of the free woman. But the son of the slave
> girl was born in the ordinary human way, whereas
> the son of the free woman was born through a promise.
> Now these things are an allegory. For these two
> women stand for two covenants. One of these covenants

—the one which originated on Mount Sinai—bears
children who are destined for slavery—and that one
is represented by Hagar. Now Hagar stands for
Mount Sinai, which is in Arabia, and corresponds
to the present Jerusalem; for she is a slave and so
are her children. But the Jerusalem which is above
is free and she is our mother. For it stands written,
" Rejoice, O barren one, who never bore a child;
break forth into a shout of joy, O you know not the
pangs of bearing a child; for the children of her who
was left alone are more than those of her who had a
husband." But we, brothers, are in the same position
as Isaac; we are children of promise. But in the old
days the child who was born in the ordinary human
way persecuted the child who was born in the spiritual
way; and exactly the same thing happens now.
But what does the scripture say? " Cast out the
slave girl and her son, for the son of the slave girl
must not inherit with the son of the free woman."
So we, brothers, are not children of the slave girl
but of the free woman. It is for this freedom that
Christ has set us free. Stand, therefore, in it and do
not get yourselves involved all over again in a slavish
yoke.

WHEN we seek to interpret a passage like this we must
always remember that for the devout and scholarly Jew,
and especially for the Rabbis, scripture had more than
one meaning; and, it is true to say, that the literal meaning
was often regarded as the least important. For the Jewish
Rabbis any passage of scripture had four meanings.
(i) *Peshat,* which was the simple or literal meaning. (ii)
Remaz, which is the suggested meaning. (iii) *Derush,*
which is the meaning evolved and deduced by investigation.
(iv) *Sod,* which was the allegorical meaning. The first
letters of these four words—P R D S—are the consonants
of the word *Paradise*—and when a man had succeeded
in penetrating into these four different meanings he reached
the joy of paradise! Now it is to be noted that the summit
and peak of all meanings was the *allegorical* meaning. It
therefore often happened that the Rabbis would take a
simple bit of historical narrative from the Old Testament

and would read into it inner meanings, which often appear to us fantastic, but which were very convincing to the people of their day. Paul was a trained Rabbi; and that is what Paul is doing here. He takes the story which involves Abraham, Sarah and Hagar, and Ishmael and Isaac (Genesis, chapters 16, 17, 21), which in the Old Testament is a straightforward narrative and allegorises it to illustrate his point.

The outline of the story is as follows:—Abraham and Sarah were far advanced in years and Sarah had no child. She did what any wife would have done in those patriarchal times, she sent Abraham in to her slave girl, Hagar, to see if she could have a child for her. Hagar had a son called Ishmael. In the meantime God had come and had promised that Sarah would have a child, which was so difficult to believe that it appeared impossible to Abraham and Sarah. But in due time the son, Isaac, was born. That is to say, Ishmael was born of the ordinary human impulses of the flesh; Isaac was born because of God's promise. And Sarah was a free woman, while Hagar was a slave girl. From the beginning Hagar had been inclined to triumph over Sarah, because barrenness was a sore shame to a woman; there was an atmosphere charged with trouble. In later days Sarah found Ishmael " mocking " Isaac—this Paul equates with persecution—and she insisted that Hagar should be cast out, for the child of the slave girl must not share the inheritance with her freeborn son. Further, Arabia was regarded as the land of slaves where the descendants of Hagar dwelt.

Paul takes that simple old story and he allegorises it. Hagar stands for the old covenant of the law, made on Mount Sinai, which is in fact in Arabia, the land of Hagar's descendants. Hagar herself was a slave and all her children were born into slavery. And that covenant whose basis is the law turns men into slaves of the law. Hagar's child was born from merely human impulses; and legalism is the best that man can do. On the other hand Sarah stands for the new covenant in Jesus Christ, God's new way of dealing with men not by law but by grace. Her child was born free and all his descendants must be free; and he was born not from any human impulse but by the promise of God. In the old story the child of the slave girl persecuted the child of the free woman; that is re-enacted in the way in which the Jews persecute the Christians, the children of law persecute the children of grace and promise. But in the end, in the old story, the child of the slave girl is cast out and has no share in the inheritance; so in the end those who are legalists will be cast out from God and cannot share in the inheritance of grace.

Strange as all this may seem to us, there remains in it the one great fact. The man who makes law the principle of his life is in the position of a slave; all his life he is seeking to satisfy his master the law. Whereas the man who makes grace the principle of his life has made love his dominant principle. He is the free man, for, as a great saint put it, the Christian principle is, " Love God and do what you like "; and it will be the power of that love, and not the constraint of law, that keeps us right; and love is always more powerful than law.

THE PERSONAL RELATIONSHIP

Galatians 5: 1-12

> Look now—it is I, Paul, who am speaking to you— I tell you that if you get yourself circumcised Christ is no good to you. Again I give my word to every man who gets himself circumcised that he is under obligation to keep the whole law. You who seek to get yourselves right with God by means of legalism have got yourself into a position in which you have rendered ineffective all that Christ did for you. You have fallen from grace. For it is by the Spirit and by faith that we eagerly expect the hope of being right with God. For in Jesus Christ it is not of the slightest importance whether a man is circumcised or uncircumcised. What does matter is faith which works

through love. You were running well. Who put up a road-block to stop you obeying the truth? The persuasion which is being exercised on you just now is not from Him who calls you. A little leaven leavens the whole lump. I have confidence in you in the Lord; I am sure that you will take no other view. He who is upsetting you—whoever he is—will bear his own judgment. As for me, brothers, if I am still preaching that circumcision is necessary, why am I still being persecuted? So the stumbling-block of the Cross is removed, is it? I wish that those who are upsetting you would get themselves not only circumcised but castrated!

IT was Paul's position that the way of grace and the way of law are mutually exclusive. The whole basic fault of the man who took the way of obedience to the law was that he assumed that something that he could do could win him merit in the eyes of God; the way of law makes salvation dependent on human achievement. On the other hand, the man who takes the way of grace simply casts himself and his sin upon the mercy of the love of God. Now Paul went on to argue that if you accepted circumcision, that is to say, if you accepted one part of the law, then logically you had to accept the whole law. Suppose that a man desires to become a naturalised subject of a country; suppose he carefully carries out all the rules and laws and regulations of that country as they affect naturalisation; then he cannot stop there; he is bound to accept *all* the other rules and laws and regulations as well. So Paul argued that if a man were circumcised he had put himself under an obligation to the whole law to which circumcision was the introduction; and, if he took that way, he had automatically turned his back on the way of grace, and, as far as he was concerned, Christ might never have died. To Paul all that mattered was faith which works through love. That is just another way of saying that the very essence of religion is not law but a personal relationship to Jesus Christ; it is the action of the heart which so loves Jesus Christ that it hands

47

itself over body and soul to Him. The Christian's faith
is never founded on a book; it is founded on a person;
its dynamic is not obedience to any law, but love to Jesus
Christ.

Once, at the beginning of things, the Galatians had
known that, but now they are turning back to the law.
" A little leaven," said Paul, " leavens the whole lump."
For the Jew leaven nearly always stood for evil influence.
What Paul is saying is, " This legalistic movement may
not have gone very far yet, but root it out before it pollutes
and destroys your whole religion."

Paul ends with an almost crudely blunt saying. Galatia
was near Phrygia and the great worship of that part of
the world was the worship of Cybele; now it was the
practice that priests and really devout worshippers of
Cybele mutilated themselves by castration. The Cybele
priests were eunuchs. So Paul says, " If you go on in
this way, of which circumcision is the beginning, you
might as well end up by castrating yourselves like these
heathen priests." It is a grim illustration at which a
polite society raises its eyebrows, but it would be intensely
real to the Galatians who knew all about the priests of
Cybele, who, in fact, lived among them.

CHRISTIAN FREEDOM

Galatians 5: 13-15

> As for you, brothers, it was for freedom that you
> were called, only you must not use this freedom as a
> bridgehead through which the worst side of human
> nature can invade you, but in love you must serve
> one another; for the whole law stands complete in
> one word, in the sentence, " You must love your
> neighbour as yourself." But if you snap at one another,
> and devour one another, you must watch that you
> do not end up by wiping each other out.

48

WITH this paragraph Paul's letter changes its emphasis. Up to this point it has been theological; and now it becomes intensely ethical. Paul had a characteristically practical mind. Even when he has been scaling the highest heights of thought he always ends a letter on a practical note. To Paul a theology was not of the slightest use unless it could be lived out in the world. So, in Romans, he wrote one of the world's great theological treatises, and then, quite suddenly, in the 12th chapter the theology comes down to earth and issues in the most practical challenge and advice. Vincent Taylor once said, " The test of a good theologian is, can he write a tract? " That is to say, after the flights of thought can he reduce all this to something that the ordinary man can understand and do? Paul always triumphantly satisfies that test. In this letter the hinge is here. The whole matter is brought to the acid test of daily life and living.

Paul's theology always ran one danger. If he declared that the end of the reign of law had come, and that the time of the reign of grace had arrived, it was always possible for some deliberate misinterpreter to say, " That, then, means that I can do what I like; that all the restraints are lifted, and I can follow my inclinations, my passions, my desires, my emotions wherever they lead me. Law is gone, and grace ensures forgiveness anyway." But to the end of the day there remained for Paul two obligations. (i) One he does not mention here, but it is implicit in all his thinking. It is *the obligation to God*. If God loved us like that then the love of Christ constrains us. I cannot soil and stain a life which God paid for with His own life. (ii) There is the *obligation to our fellow men*. We are free, but that freedom is a freedom which loves its neighbour as itself. The names of the different forms of government are suggestive. *Monarchy* is government by one, and began in the interests of efficiency, for government by committees has always had its drawbacks. *Oligarchy* means government by the few and can be justified by arguing that only the few are fit to govern. *Aristocracy* means government by the best, but the word *best* is left to be defined. *Plutocracy* means government by the wealthy and is justified by the claim that those who have the biggest stake in the country have a logical right to rule it. But *democracy* means government of the people, by the people, for the people. Now Christianity is the only true democracy, because in a Christian state everyone would think as much of his neighbour as he does of himself. Christian freedom is not licence for the simple but tremendous reason that the Christian is not the man who has become free to sin, but the man, who, by the grace of God, has become free *not to sin*. The Christian is the man who through the indwelling Spirit of Christ is so purged of self that he loves his neighbour as himself, a thing which is not possible except for a Christian.

In the end Paul adds a grim bit of advice. " Unless," he says, " you solve the problem of living together you will make life impossible and unlivable at all." Selfishness in the end does not exalt a man; it destroys him.

THE EVIL THINGS

Galatians 5: 16-21

> I tell you, let your walk and conversation be dominated by the Spirit, and don't let the desires of the lower side of your nature have their way. For the desires of the lower side of human nature are the very reverse of the desires of the Spirit, and the desires of the Spirit are the very reverse of those of the lower side of human nature, for these are fundamentally opposed to each other, so that you cannot do whatever you like. The deeds of the lower side of human nature are obvious—fornication, impurity, wantonness, idolatry, witchcraft, enmity, strife, jealousy, uncontrolled temper, self-seeking, dissension, heretical division, envy, drunkenness, carousing, and all that is like these things. I warn you, as I have warned you before, that those who do things like that will not inherit the Kingdom of God.

No man was ever more conscious of the tension in human nature than Paul. As the soldier in Studdert Kennedy's poem said;

> I'm a man and a man's a mixture
> Right down from his very birth;
> For part of him comes from heaven,
> And part of him comes from earth.

For Paul it was essential that Christian freedom and liberty should mean not freedom to indulge this lower side of human nature, but freedom to walk in the life of the Spirit. Here Paul gives us a catalogue of evil things. Every word he uses has a picture behind it, and we must look at each word separately. *Fornication*; it has been said, and said truly, that the one completely new virtue which Christianity brought into the world was chastity. Christianity came into a world where sexual immorality was not only condoned, but was regarded as normal and essential to the ordinary working of life. *Impurity*; the word that Paul uses (*akatharsia*) is an interesting word. It can be used for the pus of an unclean wound, for a tree that has never been pruned, for material which has never been sifted. In its positive form (*katharos*, an adjective meaning *pure*) it is commonly used in housing contracts to describe a house that is left clean and in good condition. But its most suggestive use is that the adjective *katharos* is used of that ceremonial cleanness which entitles a man to approach his gods. Impurity, then, is that which makes a man unfit to come before God. It is the very opposite of that purity which can see God. It is the soiling of life with the things which separate us from God. *Wantonness*; this word (*aselgeia*) has two translations in the Authorized Version. It is translated *lasciviousness* in Mark 7: 22; 2 Corinthians 12: 21; Galatians 5: 19; Ephesians 4: 29; 1 Peter 4: 3; Jude 4; and *wantonness* in Romans 13: 13 and 2 Peter 2: 18. It has been defined as " readiness for any pleasure." The man who practises it has been said to know no restraint, but to do whatever caprice and

wanton insolence may suggest. Josephus ascribed it to
Jezebel when she built a temple to Baal in Jerusalem,
the Holy City. The whole idea is the idea of a man who
is so far gone in lust and desire that he has ceased to care
what people say or think. *Idolatry;* this word means the
worship of gods which the hands of men have made. It is the
sin in which material things have taken the place of God.
Witchcraft; this word literally means *the use of drugs*.
It can be used for the beneficent use of drugs as a doctor
uses them; but it can also mean *poisoning*, and it came
to be very specially connected with the use of drugs for
witchcraft and sorcery of which the ancient world was
full. *Enmity;* the idea is that of the man who is characteristically hostile to his fellow men; it is the precise opposite
of the Christian virtue of love for the brethren and for
all men. *Strife;* originally this word had mainly to do with
the rivalry for prizes. It can even be used in a good sense in
that connection, but much more commonly it means the
rivalry which has found its outcome in contentions and
quarrellings and wrangling. *Jealousy;* this word (*zelos*
from which our word *zeal* comes) was originally a good
word. It meant *emulation*, the fine desire to share nobility
and to attain to it when we see it. But it degenerated,
and it came to mean the desire to have what someone else
has; the wrong desire for that which is not for us. *Uncontrolled temper;* the word that Paul uses means bursts and
blazes of temper. It does not describe an anger which
lasts but the anger which flames out and then dies. *Self-
seeking;* this word has a very illuminating history. It
is the word *eritheia*, and originally meant *the work of a hired
labourer* (*erithos*). So it comes to mean *work which is done
for pay*. It then goes on to mean *canvassing for political
or public office*, and it describes the man who wants office,
not from any motives of service, but for what he can get
out of it. It is the quality of the man who is essentially
self-seeking and who has no conception or idea of serving
his fellow men. *Dissension;* literally the word means

a standing apart. After one of his great victories Nelson attributed it to the fact that he had the happiness to command a band of brothers. *Dissension* describes a society in which the very opposite is the case, a society where the members fly apart instead of coming together. *Heretical division;* this might be described as crystallized dissension. The word is *hairesis,* from which comes our word *heresy. Hairesis* was not originally a bad word at all. It comes from a root which means *to choose,* and it was used for a philosopher's school of followers or for any band of people who shared a common belief. But the tragedy of life is that people who hold different views very often finish up by disliking, not each others' views, but each other. It should be possible to differ with a man and yet remain friends. *Envy;* this word (*phthonos*), is a mean word. Euripides called it " the greatest of all diseases among men." The essence of it is that it does not describe the spirit which desires, nobly or ignobly, to have what someone else has; it describes the spirit which grudges the fact that the other person has these things at all. It does not so much want the things for itself: it merely wants to take them from the other person. The Stoics defined it as "grief at someone else's good." Basil called it " grief at your neighbour's good fortune." It is the quality, not so much of the jealous, but rather of the embittered mind. *Drunkenness;* in the ancient world this was not a common vice. The Greeks drank more wine than they did milk. Even children drank wine. But they drank their wine in the proportion of three parts of water to two of wine. Greek and Christian alike would have condemned drunkenness as a thing which turned a man into a beast. *Carousing;* this word (*komos*) has an interesting history. A *komos* was a band of friends who accompanied a victor of the games after his victory. They danced and laughed and sang his praises. It also described the bands of the devotees of Bacchus the god of wine. It describes what in regency England would have been called a *rout.*

It means unrestrained and uncontrolled revelry, enjoyment that has degenerated into licence.

When we really get to the root meaning of these words we see that life has not changed so very much.

THE LOVELY THINGS

Galatians 5: 22-26

> But the fruit of the Spirit is love, joy, peace, patience, kindness, goodness, fidelity, gentleness, self-control. There is no law which condemns things like that. Those who belong to Jesus Christ have crucified their own unregenerate selves along with all their passions and their desires.
>
> If we are living in the Spirit let us also keep step with the Spirit. Don't become seekers after empty reputation; don't provoke each other; don't envy each other.

JUST as in the previous verses Paul set out the evil things which are characteristic of the flesh, so now he sets out the lovely things which are the fruit of the Spirit. Again, it is worth while to look at each word separately. *Love*; the New Testament word for *love* is *agape*. This is not a word which classical Greek uses at all commonly. In Greek there are four words for love. (*a*) *Eros* means the love of a man for a maid; it is the love which has passion in it. It is never used in the New Testament at all. (*b*) *Philia* is the warm love which we feel for our nearest and our dearest; it is a thing of the heart and the feelings of the heart. (*c*) *Storge* rather means affection and is specially used of the love of parents and children. (*d*) *Agape* the Christian word really means unconquerable benevolence. It means that no matter what a man may do to us by way of insult or injury or humiliation we will never seek anything else but his highest good. It is therefore a feeling of the mind as much as it is of the heart; it concerns the will just as much as it does the emotions.

It describes the deliberate effort—which we can only make with the help of God—never to seek anything but the best, even for those who seek the worst for us. *Joy;* the Greek word is *chara,* and the characteristic of this word is that it most often describes that joy which has a basis in religion and whose real foundation is God. (cp. Psalm 30: 11; Romans 14; 17 ; 15: 13 ; Philippians 1 : 4, 25). It is not the joy that comes from earthly things or cheap triumphs; still less is it the joy that comes from triumphing over someone else in rivalry or competition. It is a joy whose basis is God. *Peace;* in the contemporary colloquial Greek this word (*eirene*) has two interesting usages. It is used of the tranquillity and serenity which a country enjoys under the just and beneficent government of a good emperor. And it is used of the good order of a town or a village. Villages had an official who was called the superintendent of the village's *eirene;* he was the keeper of the public peace. Usually in the New Testament *eirene* stands for the Hebrew *shalom,* and means not just freedom from trouble, but rather everything that makes for a man's highest and best good. Here it means that tranquil serenity of heart which comes of the all-pervading consciousness that our times are in the hands of God. It is interesting to note that *Chara* and *Eirene* both became very common Christian names in the Church. *Makrothumia;* this is a supremely great word. The writer of First Maccabees (8: 4) says that it was by *makrothumia* that the Romans became masters of the world, and by that he means the Roman persistence which would never make peace with an enemy even in defeat, a kind of conquering patience. Generally speaking the word is not used of patience in regard to things or events, but of patience in regard to people. Chrysostom said that it is the grace of the man who could revenge himself and who does not, of the man who is slow to wrath. The most illuminating thing about it is that it is very commonly used in the New Testament of the attitude of God and of Jesus towards men. (Romans

2: 4; 9: 22; I Timothy I: 18; I Peter 3: 20). If God had been a man He would have taken His hand and wiped out this world long ago; but God has that patience which bears with all our sinning and which will not cast us off. In our lives, in our attitude to and dealings with our fellow men we must reproduce this loving, forbearing, forgiving, patient attitude of God towards ourselves.

Kindness and *goodness* are very closely connected words. For *kindness* the word is *chrestotes*. It, too, is quite commonly translated *goodness*. But sometimes the Authorised Version translates it *kindness* and sometimes *gentleness*. (Titus 3: 4; Romans 2: 4; 2 Corinthians 6: 6; Ephesians 2: 7; Colossians 3: 12; Galatians 5: 22). The Rheims version in 2 Corinthians 6: 6 translates it *sweetness*. It is a lovely word. Plutarch says that it has a far wider place than justice. Old wine is called *chrestos, mellow*. Christ's yoke is called *chrestos* (Matthew 11: 30), that is, it does not chafe and irk and gall. The whole idea of the word is a goodness which is kind. The word which Paul uses for *goodness (agathosune)* is a peculiarly Bible word and does not occur in secular Greek. (Romans 15: 14; Ephesians 5: 9; 2 Thessalonians I: 11). It is the widest word for goodness; it is defined as " virtue equipped at every point." What is the difference? *Agathosune* might, and could, rebuke and correct and discipline; *chrestotes* can only help. Trench says that Jesus showed *agathosune* when he cleansed the Temple and drove out those who were making it a bazaar; but he showed *chrestotes* when He was kind to the sinning woman who anointed His feet. The Christian needs that goodness which at one and the same time can be kind and strong. *Fidelity;* this word is common in secular Greek for *trustworthiness*. It is the characteristic of the man who is reliable. *Gentleness; praotes* is the most untranslatable of words. In the New Testament it has three main meanings. (a) It means *submissive to the will of God*. (Matthew 5: 5; 11: 29; 21: 5). (b) It means *teachable*, the man who is not too

56

proud to learn. (James 1: 21). (c) Most often of all it means *considerate*. (I Corinthians 4: 21; 2 Corinthians 10: 1; Ephesians 4: 2). Aristotle defined *praotes* as the mean between excessive anger and excessive angerlessness, as the quality of the man who is always angry at the right time and never at the wrong time. That which throws most light on its meaning is that the adjective *praus* is used of an animal who has been tamed and brought under control; and so the word speaks of that self-mastery and self-control which Christ alone can give. *Praotes* speaks of the spirit which is submissive to God, teachable in all good things, and considerate to its fellow men. *Self-control*; the word is *egkrateia*; Plato uses it of *self-mastery*. It is the spirit which has mastered its desires and its love of pleasure. It is used of the athlete's discipline of his body (I Corinthians 9: 25) and of the Christian's mastery of sex (I Corinthians 7: 9). Secular Greek uses it of the virtue of an Emperor who never lets his private interests influence the government of his people. It is the virtue which makes a man so master of himself that he is fit to be the servant of others.

It was Paul's belief and experience that the Christian died with Christ and rose again to a life, new and clean, in which the evil things of the old self are gone and the lovely things of the Spirit have come to fruition.

BURDEN-BEARING

Galatians 6: 1-5

> Brothers, if a man is caught out in some moral slip-up, you whose lives are dominated by the Spirit must correct such a man with the spirit of gentleness, and, as you do it, you must think about yourselves, in case you too should be tempted. Carry one another's burdens, and so fulfil the law of Christ. For, if anyone thinks of himself as important while he is of no importance he is deceiving himself with the fancies of his mind. Let every man test his own work, and then any ground of boasting that he has, will be in

regard to himself and not in comparison with others.
For each man must carry his own pack.

PAUL knew the problems that arise in any Christian society.
The best of men may slip up. The word that Paul uses
(*paraptoma*) does not mean a deliberate sin; but a slip
as might come to a man on an icy road or a dangerous
path. Now, the danger of those who are spiritual, and
who are really trying to live the Christian life, is that
they are very apt to judge the sins of others hardly. There
is an element of hardness in many a good man. There
are many good people to whom you could not go and sob
out a story of failure and defeat and mistake. They would
be bleakly unsympathetic. But Paul says that if a man
does make a slip the real Christian duty is to get him on
his feet again. The word that Paul uses for *to correct* is a
word that is used for executing a repair, and it is also
used for the work of a surgeon in removing some growth
from a man's body, or in setting a broken limb. The whole
atmosphere of the word lays the stress, not on punishment,
but on cure; the correction is not thought of as a penalty
but as an amendment. And Paul goes on to say that
when we see a man fall into a fault or sin we would do
well to say, " There but for the grace of God go I."

Paul goes on to rebuke conceit. He gives a recipe whereby
conceit may well be avoided. We are to compare our
achievement not with the work of our neighbours, but
with what we might have and could have done had we
done our ideal best. We may be quite cheerful about our
achievement if we compare ourselves with other people;
but when we compare it with the ideal there can never
be any cause for conceit.

Twice in this passage Paul speaks about bearing burdens.
There is a kind of burden which falls on a man which comes
from the chances and the changes of life; it comes to
him from outside; some crisis, some emergency, some
sorrow may descend upon him. It is fulfilling the law of
Christ to help everyone who is up against it. But there is a

burden which a man must bear himself. The word which Paul uses is the word for a soldier's pack. There is a duty which none can do for us and a task for which we are personally responsible. There are things which no one, however kind, can do for us, and which, however much we want to, we cannot push off on to someone else.

KEEPING IT UP

Galatians 6: 6-10

> He who is being instructed in the word must share in all good things with him who is giving instruction. Don't deceive yourselves; no one can make a fool of God; whatever a man sows this he will also reap. He who sows to his own lower nature will from that nature reap a blighted harvest. He who sows to the Spirit will from the Spirit reap life eternal. Don't get tired of doing the fine thing, for, when the proper time comes, we will reap so long as we don't relax our efforts. So then, as we have opportunity, let us do good to all, especially to those who are members of the household of the faith.

HERE Paul becomes intensely practical.

The Christian Church had its teachers. In those days the Church was a really and truly sharing institution. It was true that no Christian could bear to have too much while others had too little. So Paul says, " If a man is teaching you the eternal truths then the least you can do is to share with him such material things as you possess."

Paul then goes on to state a grim truth. He insists that in the end life holds the scales with an even and a scrupulous balance. If a man allows the lower side of his nature to dominate him, in the end he can expect nothing but a harvest of trouble. But if a man keeps on always walking the high way, and always doing the fine thing, he may have to wait long, but in the end God repays. Christianity never took the threat out of life. The Greeks believed in Nemesis; they believed that, when a man did a wrong thing, immediately Nemesis was on his trail and sooner or later would catch up. All Greek tragedy is a sermon on the text, " The doer shall suffer." What we do not sufficiently remember is this—it is true, and blessedly true, that God can and does forgive men for their sins; but not even God can wipe out the consequence of sin. If a man sins against his body soon or late he will pay in ruined health—even if he is forgiven. If a man sins against his loved ones soon or late hearts will be broken—even if he is forgiven. John B. Gough, the great temperance orator, who had lived a reckless early life, used to declare in warning, " The scars remain." And Origen, the great Christian scholar, who was a universalist, believed that all men would be saved but that even then the marks of sin would remain. We must remember that we cannot trade on the forgiveness of God; there is a moral law in the universe and if a man breaks it he will be forgiven, but nonetheless, he breaks it at his peril.

So Paul finishes by reminding his friends that sometimes the duty and the task of charity and generosity may be wearisome and irksome; but that duty remains; and no man who ever cast his bread upon the waters found that it did not return some day to him.

THE CLOSING WORDS

Galatians 6: 11-18

> See in what large letters I am writing in my own handwriting. Those who wish to make a pretentious display from the merely human point of view are trying to compel you to get yourselves circumcised, but their real object is to avoid persecution because of the Cross of Christ. For those who advocate circumcision do not themselves keep the law, but they wish you to get yourselves circumcised that they may boast about the way in which you are observing the outward and the human rituals. God forbid that I should boast except in the Cross of our Lord Jesus Christ through whom the world has been crucified to me and I to the world. To be circumcised is of no importance, and to be uncircumcised makes no

difference. What does matter is to be re-created.
May peace and mercy be upon all who shall walk
by this standard and on the Israel of God. For the
future, let no one trouble me for I bear the brands of
Jesus in my body.

Brothers, the grace of the Lord Jesus Christ be
with your spirit. So let it be.

ORDINARILY Paul only added his signature to the letter
which the scribe wrote to his dictation; but in this case
his heart is running over with such love and anxiety for
the Galatians that he writes this whole last paragraph.
" See," he says, " in what large letters I am writing in
my own handwriting." The large letters may be due to
three things. (*a*) This paragraph may be written large
because of its importance, as if it were printed in heavy
type. (*b*) It may be written large because Paul was unused
to wielding a pen and it was the best that he could do.
(*c*) It may be that Paul's eyes were weak, or that the blind-
ing headache was on him, and all he could produce was
the large sprawling handwriting of a man who can hardly see.

Once more he comes back to the centre of the matter.
Those who want the Galatians to get themselves circumcised do so for three reasons. (*a*) It would save them from
persecution. The Romans recognized the Jewish religion
and officially allowed Jews to practise it. Circumcision
was the unanswerable mark of a Jew. And so these people
saw in circumcision a passport to safety should persecution
arise. Persecution would keep them safe from the hatred
of the Jews and the law of Rome alike. (*b*) In the last
analysis, by circumcision, and by keeping of the rules
and regulations of the law, they were trying to put on a
show that would win the approval of God. Paul was quite
certain that nothing that man can do can win salvation;
so once again he points them to the Cross whereon the
grace and love of God are full displayed. He summons
them to cease trying to earn salvation and to trust to
the grace which loved them like that. (*c*) Those who
desired the Galatians to be circumcised did not themselves

keep the law. No man could keep it all. But they wanted to boast about the Galatians as their latest converts and trophies. They wanted to glory in their power over the people whom they had reduced to their own legalistic slavery. And so Paul once again lays it down with all the intensity of which he is capable that circumcision and uncircumcision do not matter; what matters is that act of faith and trust in Christ which opens a new life to a man and which creates him all over again.

" I bear," said Paul, " the brands of Jesus in my body." There are two possible meanings of this. (*a*) The *stigmata* have always fascinated men. It is told of Francis of Assisi that once as he fasted on a lonely mountain top he seemed to see the love of God crucified on a Cross that stretched across the whole horizon; as he saw it a sword of grief and pity pierced his heart. Slowly the vision faded and Francis relaxed; and then, they say, he looked down and lo! the marks of the nails were in his hands and he bore them to the end of his days. Whether it is truth or legend we cannot tell, for there are more things in this world than our matter-of-fact philosophy dreams of. There are some who think that Paul had so really passed through an experience of crucifixion with his Lord that he too bore the print of the nails on his hands. (*b*) Often a master branded his slaves with a mark that showed them to be his. Most likely what Paul means is that the scars and marks of the things he had suffered for Christ are the brands which show him to be the slave of Christ. In the end it is not his apostolic authority that he uses as a basis of appeal; it is the wounds he bore for Christ's sake. Like Mr. Valiant-for-Truth Paul said, " My marks and scars I carry with me to be my witness to Him who will now be my rewarder."

And so after the storm and stress and tensity of the letter there comes the peace of the benediction. Paul has argued and rebuked and cajoled but his last word is GRACE, for him the only word that mattered.

THE LETTER TO
THE EPHESIANS

The Rev. WILLIAM BARCLAY, D.D.

First Edition - *March,* 1956
Second Edition - *September,* 1958
Second Impression - *September,* 1960

To ALL THE STUDENTS OF TRINITY COLLEGE
WHOM IT HAS BEEN MY PRIVILEGE TO TEACH
AND WHO ARE NOW ENGAGED UPON THE WORK
OF THE CHURCH AT HOME
AND
OF THE YOUNGER CHURCHES OVERSEAS.

FOREWORD

As I have begun all other volumes in this series, so I must begin this one with an expression of my very sincere thanks to the Publications Committee of the Church of Scotland for allowing me to continue with this series, and above all to the Committee's Secretary and Manager, the Rev. Andrew McCosh, M.A., S.T.M., and to the Committee's Convener, the Rev. R. G. Macdonald, O.B.E., D.D., for their constant patience and help and encouragement.

This present volume contains one of the most frequently studied letters of Paul, *The Letter to the Ephesians*. The *Letter to the Ephesians* must always remain one of Paul's most important letters, for in it Paul gives to us his doctrine and his ideal of the Church.

Ephesians has been fortunate in its commentators. On the Greek text of *Ephesians* there are three great commentaries, those by J. Armitage Robinson, B. F. Westcott, and T. K. Abbott in the International Critical Commentary. On the English text there is another version of J. Armitage Robinson's commentary, that by E. F. Scott in the Moffatt Commentary, and that by H. G. C. Moule in the Cambridge Bible for Schools and Colleges, which is now old, but still of very great value. There is also a recent most excellent exposition of *Ephesians* by Dr. John A. Mackay entitled *God's Order*. All these works have been in constant use.

As I have said in the case of previous volumes in this series, the translation given claims no special merit, and was included mainly in order that the reader might be able to read and study the book anywhere.

In *Ephesians* we have set before us the ideal of the Church. It is my hope and my prayer that this volume of studies may do something to enable us to realize more clearly the greatness of the Church to which we belong, and the height of the Christian life which we are called upon to live.

WILLIAM BARCLAY.

TRINITY COLLEGE,
    GLASGOW.
        February, 1956.

INTRODUCTION

The Supreme Letter

By common consent the *Letter to the Ephesians* ranks
very high in the devotional and theological literature of
the Christian Church. It has been called " The Queen of
the Epistles "—and rightly so. There are many who
would hold that it is indeed the highest reach of New
Testament thought. When John Knox was dying, and
when he was very near the end, the book that was most
often read to him was John Calvin's *Sermons on the Letter
to the Ephesians.* Coleridge, the great poet and philosopher,
said of *Ephesians* that it was " the divinest composition
of man." He went on: " It embraces first, those doctrines
peculiar to Christianity, and, then, those precepts common
with it in natural religion." *Ephesians* is clearly a
letter which has a place all its own in the Pauline correspondence.

And yet, although that is the case, there are certain
very real problems connected with *Ephesians,* and these
problems are not the production of the minds of over-
critical scholars; they are problems which are plain for
all to see. But it is also true that, when these problems
are solved, *Ephesians* becomes a greater letter than ever,
and shines with an even more radiant light, and is clad
with an even greater importance.

The Circumstances of the Writing of Ephesians

Before we turn to any of the doubtful things, let us
first set down the certainties. First, *Ephesians* was clearly
written when Paul was in prison. He calls himself " the
prisoner of Christ " (3: 1); it is as " the prisoner of God "
that he beseeches them (4: 1); he is, in his own famous
phrase, " an ambassador in bonds " (6: 20). It was in
prison, and very near to the end, that Paul wrote *Ephesians.*
Second, *Ephesians* has very clearly a very close and intimate

71

connection with *Colossians*. It would seem that Tychicus was the bearer of both these letters, for in *Colossians* Paul says that Tychicus will declare all his state to them (*Colossians* 4: 7); and in *Ephesians* he says that Tychicus will give them all information about his affairs and how he is faring (*Ephesians* 6: 20). Tychicus is intimately connected with both these letters. But further, there is a very close resemblance between the substance of the two letters. So close is this resemblance that there are more than 55 verses in the two letters which are verbatim the same. Either, as Coleridge held, *Colossians* is what might be called " the overflow " of *Ephesians*, or *Ephesians* is another and a greater version of *Colossians*. We shall in the end come to see that it is this resemblance which gives us the clue to the unique place of *Ephesians* among the letters of Paul.

The Problem

So, then, it is certain that *Ephesians* was written when Paul was in prison for the faith, and that *Ephesians* has in some way the closest possible connection with *Colossians*. Wherein then lies the problem? The problem emerges when we begin to examine the question of *to whom Ephesians was written*. In the ancient days letters were written on rolls of papyrus. When they were finished, they were tied with thread, and, if they were specially private or important, the knots in the thread were then sealed. But it was seldom that any address was written on them, for the very simple reason that, for the ordinary individual, there was no postal system in the ancient world. There was a government post, but it was only available for official and imperial correspondence, and was not available for the ordinary person and for his letters. Letters in those days were delivered by hand; they were given to someone to deliver personally; and therefore no address was necessary. So the titles of the New Testament letters are not part of the original letters at all. They were inserted afterwards when the letters were collected and published for all the Church to read.

Now, when we study the *Letter to the Ephesians* closely and intelligently, we find that it is in fact in the last degree unlikely that it was written to the Church at Ephesus. There are *internal* reasons for arriving at that conclusion. (*a*) It is clear that the letter was written to Gentiles. The recipients of the letter were " Gentiles in the flesh, called the uncircumcision by those of the circumcision, without Christ, aliens from the commonwealth of Israel, and strangers from the covenants of promise " (2: 11). Paul beseeches them " not to walk as other Gentiles walk " (4: 17). The fact that they were Gentiles would not, of course, mean that the letter was not written to Ephesus; but that is the fact about the recipients of the letter which is certain. (*b*) It is undeniable that *Ephesians* is the most impersonal letter that Paul ever wrote. There is not a personal touch in it from beginning to end. It is entirely without personal greetings, and without the intimate personal messages of which the other letters are so full. That is doubly surprising when we remember that Paul spent longer in Ephesus than in any other city; he spent no less than three years in Ephesus (*Acts* 18: 9, 10). Further, in *Acts* 20: 17-35 we have Paul's farewell talk to the elders of Ephesus, before he left Miletus on his last journey. There is no more intimate and affectionate passage in the whole New Testament; and it is very difficult to believe in face of all that that Paul would have sent a letter to Ephesus which was completely impersonal and without any intimacies at all. (*c*) Still further, the indication of the letter is that Paul and the recipients did not know each other personally, that their knowledge of each other came by hearsay and by report, and not by actual contact. In 1: 15 Paul writes: " After I had *heard* of your faith in the Lord Jesus." The loyalty of the people to whom he was writing was something which had come to him by information and not by experience. In 3: 2 he writes to them: " If you have heard of the dispensation that God gave me in regard to you." That is to say: " If you have heard that God gave me the special task and office of being the apostle to Gentiles such as you." The Church's knowledge of Paul, in this case, as the apostle to the Gentiles was something of which they have heard, but not something which they knew by personal contact with him. So, then, within itself, the letter bears signs that it does not fit the close and personal relationship which Paul had with the Church at Ephesus.

These facts might be accounted for or explained away; but there is one external fact which settles the matter. In 1: 1 none of the great early manuscripts of the Greek New Testament contain the words *in Ephesus*. The great manuscripts all read: " Paul . . . to all those who are saints and faithful in Christ Jesus." And we know, from the way in which they comment on it, that was in fact the form in which the great early Greek fathers knew the first verse of *Ephesians*.

Was Paul the Author ?

There are some scholars who have gone on to find still another difficulty in *Ephesians*. They have doubted whether Paul was the author of the letter at all. On what grounds, then, do they base their doubts? They say that the *vocabulary* is different from the vocabulary of Paul; and it is true that there are some seventy words in *Ephesians* which are not found in any other letter written by Paul. That need not trouble us, for the fact is that in *Ephesians* Paul was saying things which he had never said before; he was travelling a road of thought along which he had not before travelled; and very naturally he needed new words to express new thoughts. It would be ridiculous to demand that a man with a mind like Paul's mind should never add to his vocabulary and should always express himself in the same way. They say that the *style* is not the style of Paul. Now it is true—we can see it even in

74

the English, let alone in the Greek—that the style of *Ephesians* is different from that of the other letters. The other letters are all written to meet a definite situation, a definite emergency, a definite set of problems. But, as A. H. M'Neile has said, *Ephesians* is " a theological tract, or rather a religious mediation." Even the use of language is different. Moffatt puts it this way—generally speaking, Paul's language pours out like a cascade and a torrent, with a perfect cataract of impassioned words; but in Ephesians we have " a slow, bright stream, flowing steadily along, which brims its high banks." The length of the sentences in *Ephesians* is astonishing. In the Greek *Ephesians* 1: 3-14, 15-23; 2: 1-9; 3: 1-7 are each one long, meandering sentence. M'Neile very beautifully and rightly calls Ephesians " a poem in prose." All this is very unlike Paul's normal style.

What, then, is to be said to this? There is first the general fact that no great writer always writes in the same style. A Shakespeare can produce the very different styles of *Hamlet*, *The Midsummer Night's Dream*, *The Taming of the Shrew* and the *Sonnets*. Any great stylist— and Paul was a great stylist—writes in a style to fit his aim and his circumstances at the time of writing. It is bad criticism to say that Paul did not write *Ephesians* simply because he has evolved a new vocabulary and a new style. But there is more than that. Let us remember how Paul wrote most of his letters. He wrote them in the midst of a busy ministry, when, for the most part, he was on the road. He wrote them to meet a clamant and demanding problem, which had to be dealt with at the moment and at once. That is to say, in most of his letters Paul was writing in very difficult circumstances, and he was writing, in almost every case, against time. Now let us remember how Paul wrote *Ephesians*. He wrote it *when he was in prison*. That is to say, he had all the time in the world to write it. He did not need to dash it off, for there were ahead of him months in prison when he had nothing else to do but to think and to write. Is it any wonder that the style of *Ephesians* is not the style of the earlier letters? Still further, this difference in style, this meditative, poetical quality is most apparent in the first three chapters, and the first three chapters are *one long prayer*, culminating in the great doxology at the end of chapter 3. There is in fact nothing like this in all Paul's letters. This is the language of lyrical prayer, not the language of argument, and controversy, and rebuke.

It is perfectly true that *Ephesians* is written with a vocabulary and in a style which differs from those of the other letters of Paul; but *Ephesians* was written to express new ideas, in very different circumstances, and—as we shall see—for a very different purpose from any of the other letters. The differences are far from proving that *Ephesians* is not by Paul.

The Thought of the Epistle

There are certain scholars who wish to go on to say that the thought of *Ephesians* is beyond the thought of any of the other letters of Paul. Let us see what the thought of *Ephesians* is. We have seen that *Ephesians* is intimately connected with *Colossians*. The great central thought of *Colossians* is *the all-sufficiency of Jesus Christ*. In Jesus Christ there dwelt all knowledge and all wisdom (*Colossians* 2: 3); it pleased the Father that in Him all fulness should dwell (*Colossians* I: 19); in that great phrase, Christ is the fulness of the Godhead bodily (*Colossians* 2: 9); He alone is necessary and sufficient for man's salvation (*Colossians* I: 14). The whole of the thought of *Colossians* is based on the complete sufficiency of Jesus Christ. The thought of *Ephesians* is a development of that conception. The whole thought of *Ephesians* is summarized in two verses of the first chapter, in which Paul speaks of God as, " having made known unto us the mystery of His will according to His good pleasure which He hath purposed in Himself, that, in the dispensation of the fulness of times,

He might gather together in one all things in Christ, both
which are in heaven and which are on earth, even in Him "
(*Ephesians* 1: 9, 10).

The key thought of *Ephesians* is the gathering together
of all things in Jesus Christ. Christ is the centre in whom
all things unite, and the bond who unites all things. In
nature as it is without Christ there is nothing but disunity
and disharmony. There is battle in nature; nature is
" red in tooth and claw." Man's dominion has broken the
social union which should exist between man and the
beasts. Man is divided from man; class from class; nation
from nation; ideology from ideology; Gentile from Jew.
The world, as we see it without Christ, is a divided, disunited, fragmented world. What is true of the world
of outer nature is true of human nature itself. In every
man there is a tension; every man is a walking civil war;
there is a constant battle between the higher and the
lower side of man; man is always torn between the desire
for good and the desire for evil; he hates his sins and loves
his sins at one and the same time. According to both
Greek and Jewish thought in the time of Paul, this battle
and this disharmony and this disunity extended even to
the heavenly places. There is a cosmic battle raging
between the powers of evil and the powers of good; between
the good and the bad spirits and angelic powers; between
God and the demons. Worst of all there is disharmony,
disunity, separation between God and man. Man, who
was meant to be in fellowship with God, is estranged
from God. So, then, in this world without Christ, wherever
we look there is nothing but disunity. That disunity is
not God's purpose; God purposed the universe to be a
harmony and not a disharmony; and this disunity can
only become a unity, and this disharmony can only become
a harmony, when all things and all men and all powers in
heaven and earth are united in Christ. As E. F. Scott
has it: " The innumerable broken strands were to be

brought together in Christ, knotted again into one, as they had been in the beginning." The central thought of *Ephesians* is the realization of disunity in nature, disunity in man, disunity in time, disunity in eternity, disunity between God and man, and the conviction that all that disunity can only become unity when all men and all powers are united in Christ.

The Origin of Paul's Thought

How did Paul arrive at this great conception of the unity of all things in Jesus Christ? Most likely he came to it in two ways. It is surely the inevitable outcome of his conviction, stated so vividly in *Colossians*, that Christ is all-sufficient. If Christ is the all-sufficient one, then all men and all things and all powers can only come to unity when they accept and live in Christ. But it may well be that there was something else which moved Paul's mind in this direction. Paul was a Roman citizen, and proud of it. In his journeys Paul had seen a great deal of the Roman Empire, and now he was in Rome, the imperial city. Now, in the Roman Empire a new unity had come to the world. The *pax Romana*, the Roman peace, was a very real thing. Kingdoms and states and countries, which had battled and struggled and competed and warred with each other, were gathered into a new unity in the Empire which was Rome. The barriers were down; the divisions were bridged; the hostilities were ended; the tensions were relaxed; all were gathered into one in Rome. It may well be that in his imprisonment Paul saw with new eyes how all this unity centred in Rome; and it may well have seemed to him a symbol and parable of how all things must centre in Christ, and be gathered together in Him, if a disunited nature and world and humanity were ever to be gathered into a unity. Surely, so far from being a conception that was beyond Paul's thinking, all Paul's thinking and experience would lead him precisely to that.

The Function of the Church

It is in the first three chapters of the letter that Paul deals with this conception of the unity in Christ. In the second three chapters he has much to say of the place of the Church in God's plan to bring about that unity. What did the Church stand for? What was the Church's true function in the plan of God? Where does the Church come in in this purpose of bringing a new united into a disunited world? It is here that Paul strikes out one of his greatest phrases. The Church is the *Body of Christ.* The Church is to be hands to do Christ's work, feet to run upon His errands, a mouth to speak for Him, an instrument, a body through which He can work. So, then, we have a double thesis in *Ephesians.* First, Christ is God's instrument of reconciliation. Second, the Church is Christ's instrument of reconciliation. The Church must bring Christ to the world; and it is within the Church that all the middle walls of partition and separation must be broken down. It is through the Church that the unity of all the discordant elements must be wrought out and achieved. It is the Church who must preach the Christ in whom unity alone is possible, and it is within the Church that this unity must be achieved and realized. As E. F. Scott has it: " The Church stands for that purpose of world-wide reconciliation for which Christ appeared, and in all their intercourse with one another Christians must seek to realize this formative idea of the Church."

Who but Paul ?

This, then, is the thought of *Ephesians.* As we have seen, there are some who, thinking of the vocabulary and the style and the thought of this letter, cannot believe that Paul wrote it. E. J. Goodspeed, the American scholar, has put forward an interesting—but unconvincing— theory. All the probability is that it was in Ephesus about the year A.D. 90 that the letters of Paul were first collected and published and sent out to the Church at large. It is

Goodspeed's theory that the man who was responsible for that collection, some disciple and lover of Paul, wrote *Ephesians* as a kind of preface and introduction to the whole collection. Surely that theory breaks down on one salient fact. Any imitation is inferior to the original. Any secondary work reveals itself as secondary. But so far from being inferior *Ephesians* might well be said to be the greatest of all the Pauline letters and, if Paul did not write it himself, we have to postulate as its writer someone who was at least as great as, and quite possibly greater than, Paul. E. F. Scott very relevantly demands: " Can we believe that in the Church of Paul's day there was an unknown teacher of this supreme excellence? The natural assumption is surely that an epistle so like the work of Paul at his best was written by no other man than by Paul himself." No man ever had a greater vision of Christ than this vision which sees in Christ the one centre in whom all the disunities of life are gathered into one. No man ever had a greater vision of the Church than the vision which sees in the Church God's instrument in that world-wide and universal reconciliation. And we may well believe that no man other than Paul could rise to a vision like that.

The Destination of Ephesians

We must now return to the problem which earlier we left unsolved. If *Ephesians* was not written to Ephesus— and we have seen that it can hardly have been so written— to what Church was it written?

The oldest suggestion is that it was written to *Laodicaea*. In *Colossians* 4: 16 Paul writes: " And when this epistle is read among you, cause that it be read also in the Church of the Laodicaeans; and that ye likewise read the epistle from Laodicaea." From that sentence it is certain that a letter had gone from Paul to the Church at Laodicaea. We possess no such letter amongst Paul's letters as they stand. Marcion was one of the first people to make a collection of Paul's letters; he made his list just about the middle of the second century, and he actually calls *Ephesians* the Letter to the Laodicaeans. So from very early times there must have been a feeling in the Church that *Ephesians* was actually sent in the first instance to Laodicaea.

If we accept that interesting and attractive suggestion, we would still have to explain how the letter lost its individual address to Laodicaea and came to be connected with Ephesus. There could be two explanations.

It may be that, when Paul died, the Church at Ephesus knew that the Church at Laodicaea possessed a very wonderful letter from Paul. It may be that the Christians of Ephesus wrote to Laodicaea asking for a copy. A copy may have been made and sent off, omitting only the words *in Laodicaea* in the first verse, and leaving a blank as the earliest manuscripts have a blank there. Almost thirty years later the letters of Paul were collected for general publication. Now Laodicaea was in a district which was notorious for earthquakes, and it may well have been that all Laodicaea's archives were destroyed; and that, therefore, when the collection was made, the only copy of the Letter to the Laodicaeans was that which survived in Ephesus. That letter may then have been included in the Pauline collection, and since it was found in Ephesus it may have come to be known as the Letter to the Ephesians, because it was in Ephesus that the only extant copy survived. That is perfectly possible.

The second suggested explanation was propounded by Harnack, the great German scholar. In the later days the Church in Laodicaea sadly fell from grace. In the *Revelation* there is a letter to Laodicaea which makes sad reading (*Revelation* 3: 14-22). In that letter the Church of Laodicaea is sadly and unsparingly condemned by the Risen Christ, so much so that He says to her in that vivid phrase: " I will spue thee out of my mouth " (*Revelation* 3: 16). Now in the ancient world there was a custom called *damnatio memoriae*, the condemnation of a man's memory. A man might have rendered many a signal service to the state, for which his name might occur in books, in the state annals, in inscriptions and on memorials. But it might be that such a man might end in some base act of treachery, some shameful dishonesty, some utter wreck of all honour. In such a case his memory was condemned. His name was erased from all books; it was obliterated from all inscriptions; it was chiselled out of all memorials. He underwent a *damnatio memoriae*. Harnack thinks it possible that the Church of Laodicaea underwent a *damnatio memoriae*, that her very name was obliterated from the Christian records. If that were so, then the copies of the Letter to Laodicaea would have no address at all; and when the collection was made at Ephesus, since the letter survived in Ephesus, the name of Ephesus might well have become attached to it, because it had no other name.

The Circular Letter

Both these suggestions are possible, but there is still another suggestion which is far more likely and which we believe to be correct. We believe that the early manuscripts of *Ephesians* have the name of no Church in them because *Ephesians was not in fact written to any one Church, but was a circular letter to all Paul's Asian Churches.* It was never the possession of one Church, but always the possession of all the Churches. Let us look again at the saying of Paul in *Colossians* 4: 16. He writes: " And when this epistle is read among you, cause that it be read also in the Church at Laodicaea; and that ye read likewise the epistle from Laodicaea." Now note Paul does not say that the Colossians must read the epistle *to* Laodicaea; they must read the epistle *from* Laodicaea. It is as if Paul said: " There is a letter circulating; at the present moment it has reached Laodicaea; when it comes to you, when it is sent on to you, from Laodicaea, be sure to read it." That sounds very like as if there was a letter circulating among the Asian Churches, and we believe that letter which was circulating throughout the Churches was *Ephesians*.

The Quintessence of Paul

If this be so, and we believe that it is so, *Ephesians* is Paul's supreme letter. We have seen that *Ephesians* and *Colossians* are very close to each other. We believe that what happened was that Paul wrote *Colossians* to deal with a definite situation and a definite outbreak of heresy. In so writing he stumbled on his great expression of the all-sufficiency of Christ. He said to himself: " This is something that I must get across to all men." So he took the matter he had used in *Colossians*; he removed all the local and the temporary and the controversial aspects of it; and he wrote a new letter to tell all men of the all-sufficient Christ. *Ephesians*, as we see it, is the one letter Paul sent to all the eastern Churches to tell them that the destined unity of all men and of all things could never be found except in Christ, and to tell them of the supreme task of the Church—the task of being Christ's instrument and body in the task of world-wide and universal reconcilation of man to man, and of man to God. That is why indeed *Ephesians* is the Queen of the Epistles.

EPHESIANS

IN the letter to the Ephesians Paul's argument is very closely woven together. It often proceeds in long complicated sentences which are very difficult to unravel. If we are really to grasp his meaning, there are sections where it will be better to read the letter as we go through it, first in fairly long sections, and then take the sections and break them down into shorter passages for detailed study.

THE PURPOSE OF GOD

EPHESIANS 1: 1-14

THIS is a letter from Paul, an apostle of Jesus Christ, through the will of God, to God's consecrated people who live in Ephesus and who are faithful in Jesus Christ. Grace be to you and peace from God our Father and from the Lord Jesus Christ.

Blessed be the God and Father of our Lord Jesus Christ, who has blessed us with all the spiritual blessings which are only to be found in heaven, even as He chose us in Him before the foundation of the world, that we might be holy and blameless before Him. He determined in His love before time began to adopt us to Himself through Jesus Christ, in the good purpose of His will, so that all might praise the glory of the generous gift which He freely gave us in the Beloved. For it is in Him that we have a deliverance which cost His life; in Him we have received the forgiveness of sins, which only the wealth of His grace could give, a grace which He gave us in abundant supply, and which conferred on us all wisdom and all sound sense. This happened because He made known to us the once hidden, but now revealed, secret of His will, for so it was His good pleasure to do. This secret was a purpose which He formed in His own mind before time began, so that the periods of time should be controlled and administered until they reached their full development, a development in which all things, in heaven and upon earth, are gathered into one in Jesus Christ. It was in Christ, in whom our portion in this scheme was also assigned to us, that it was determined, by the decision of Him who controls everything according to the purpose of His will, that we, who were the first to set our hopes upon the coming of the Anointed One of God, should become the means whereby His glory should be praised. And it was in Christ that it was determined that you, too, should become the means whereby God's glory is praised, after you had heard the word which brings the truth, the good news of your salvation—that good news, in which, after you had come to believe, you were sealed with the Holy Spirit, who had been promised to you, the Spirit who is the foretaste and guarantee of all that one day we will inherit, until we enter into that complete redemption which brings complete possession.

GREETINGS TO GOD'S PEOPLE

Ephesians I: I, 2

> This is a letter from Paul, an apostle of Jesus Christ, through the will of God, to God's consecrated people who live in Ephesus and who are faithful in Jesus Christ. Grace be to you, and peace from God our Father and from the Lord Jesus Christ.

PAUL begins his letter with the only two claims to fame which he possessed. (i) He was *an apostle of Christ.* When Paul said that there were three things in his mind. (*a*) He meant that he *belonged* to Christ. His life was not his own to do with as he liked; he was the possession of Jesus Christ, and he must always live, not as he wanted to live, but as Jesus Christ wanted him to live. (*b*) He meant that he was *commissioned* and sent out by Jesus Christ. The word *apostolos* comes from the verb *apostellein,* which means *to despatch* or *to send out.* It can be used, for instance, of a naval squadron sent out on an expedition; it can be used of an ambassador sent out by his native country. It describes a man who is sent out with some special task to do. The Christian all through life sees himself as a member of the task force of Christ. The Christian is a man with a mission, the mission of serving Christ within this world. (*c*) He meant that *any power he possessed was a delegated power.* The Sanhedrin was the supreme court of the Jews. In matters of religion the Sanhedrin had authority over every Jew throughout the world. When the Sanhedrin came to a decision, that decision was given to an *apostolos*, that the *apostolos* might convey it to the persons whom it concerned, and that he might see that it was carried out. When such an *apostolos* went out, he did not go out simply in his own authority and in his own strength. Behind him, and in him, there lay the authority of the Sanhedrin, whose representative he was. The Christian is the representative of Christ within the world, but he is not left to carry out that task in his own strength and power; the strength and power of Jesus Christ are with him. (ii) Paul goes on to say that he was an apostle *through the will of God*. When Paul said that, the accent in his voice was not the accent of pride, it was the accent of sheer amazement. To the end of the day Paul stood amazed that God could have chosen a man like him to do His work.

> ' How Thou canst think so well of us,
>   And be the God Thou art,
> Is darkness to my intellect,
>   But sunshine to my heart."

A Christian must never be filled with pride in any task that God gives him to do; he must be filled with wondering amazement that God thought him worthy of a share in His work.

So Paul goes on to address his letter to the people who live in Ephesus and who are faithful in Jesus Christ. The Christian is a man who always lives a double life. Paul's friends were people who lived *in Ephesus* and *in Christ*. Every Christian has a human address and a divine address. He lives in a certain place in this world, but he also lives in Christ. And that is precisely the secret of the Christian life. Alister MacLean tells of a lady in the West Highlands who lived a hard life, yet a life of perpetual serenity. When she was asked the secret of it, she answered: " My secret is to sail the seas, and always to keep my heart in port." The secret of the Christian serenity is that wherever the Christian is, he is still in Christ.

Paul begins with the greeting with which he always begins. " Grace be to you," he says, " and peace." Here are the two great words of the Christian faith. The word *grace* has always two main ideas in it. Grace is always something lovely. The Greek word is *charis*, and *charis* in English could mean *charm*. There must be a certain loveliness, a certain charm, in the Christian life. A Christianity which is unattractive is no real Christianity. Grace always describes a gift, and a gift which it would have been impossible for a man to procure for himself, and which he never earned and in no way deserved. God's treatment of us, God's gifts to us are things which came to us out of the sheer generosity of the heart of God. Whenever we mention the word grace we must think of the sheer loveliness of the Christian life, and the sheer undeserved generosity of the heart of God. When we think of the word *peace* in connection with the Christian life we must be careful. In Greek the word is *eirēnē*, but it translates the Hebrew word *shalōm*. In the Bible the word *peace* is never a purely negative word; it never describes simply the absence of trouble and hardship and distress. *Shalōm* means everything which makes for a man's highest good, everything which is calculated to make him a man in the highest sense of the term, everything which is calculated to make life truly worth living. This Christian peace is something which is quite independent of outward circumstances. A man might live in ease and luxury and on the fat of the land; he might have the finest of houses and the biggest of bank accounts, and yet not have peace; on the other hand, a man might be starving in prison, or dying at the stake, or living a life from which all comfort had fled, and be at perfect peace. What is the explanation of it? The explanation is that there is only one source of peace in all the world, and that is doing the will of God. We know perfectly well that when in life we are doing something which we know we ought not to do, or when we are evading something that we know we ought

87

to do, there is always a haunting uneasiness and dispeace at the back of our minds; and we know quite well that even if we are doing something very difficult, even if we are doing something which we do not want to do, if we know that it is the right thing there is a certain contentment in our hearts. " In His will is our peace." The only peace on earth is in the will of God.

THE CHOSEN OF GOD

Ephesians I: 3, 4

> Blessed be the God and Father of our Lord Jesus Christ, who has blessed us with all the spiritual blessings which are only to be found in heaven, even as He chose us in Him before the foundation of the world, that we might be holy and blameless before Him.

IN the Greek the long passage from verse 3 to verse 14 is one single sentence. It is so long and so complicated because it represents not so much a reasoned statement as a lyrical song of praise. Paul's mind goes on and on, not because he is thinking in logical stages, but because gift after gift and wonder after wonder from God pass before his eyes and enter into his mind. To understand it we must break it up and take it in short sections.

In this passage Paul is thinking of the Christians as the chosen people of God, and his mind runs along three lines.

(i) He thinks of the *fact of God's choice*. Paul never thought of himself as having chosen to serve God and to do God's work. He always thought of God as having chosen him. Jesus said to His disciples: " Ye have not chosen me, but I have chosen you " (*John* 15: 16). To Paul everything was of God; and herein precisely lies the wonder. It would not be so wonderful that man should choose God; the wonder is that God should choose man.

(ii) Paul thinks of *the bounty of God's choice*. God chose us to bless us with these blessings which are only to be found in heaven. There are certain things which a man can find and discover for himself; but there are other things which are beyond his obtaining. A man by himself can attain to a certain skill in a craft or science; he can attain to a certain position in the world; he can amass a certain amount of this world's goods. But by himself he can never attain to goodness or to peace of mind. God chose us to give us those things which He alone can give.

(iii) Paul thinks of *the purpose of God's choice*. God chose us that we should be *holy* and *blameless*. Here are two great words. The word *holy* is the Greek word *hagios*. The word *hagios* always has in it the idea of *difference* and of *separation*. A thing which is *hagios* is *different* from ordinary things. A temple is *holy* because it is different from other buildings; a priest is *holy* because he is different from ordinary men; a victim is *holy* because it is different from other animals; God is supremely *holy* because God is different from men; the Sabbath day is *holy* because it is different from other days. So, then, God chose the Christian that he should be *different* from other men. Here is the fact and the challenge that the modern Church has been very slow to face. In the early Church the Christian never had any doubt that he must be different from the world; he, in fact, knew that he must be so different that the probability was that the world would kill him, and the certainty was that the world would hate him. But the tendency in the modern Church has been to play down the difference between the Church and the world. We have, in effect, so often said to people: " So long as you go on living a decent, respectable life, it is quite all right to become a Church member and to call yourself a Christian. You don't need to be so very different from other people." In point of fact a Christian should be identifiable in the world. It must always be remembered that this difference on which Christ insists is not a difference which takes a man *out* of the world; it makes him different *within* the world. It should be possible to identify the Christian in the school, the shop, the factory, the office, the hospital ward, everywhere. And the difference is this—that the Christian lives and works and behaves, not as any human laws compel him so to do, but as the law of Christ compels him to do. A Christian teacher is not out to satisfy the regulations of an education authority or a headmaster; he is out to satisfy the demands of Christ, and that will almost certainly mean a very different attitude to the pupils under his charge. A Christian workman is not out to satisfy the regulations of a Trades Union, but of Jesus Christ, which will certainly make him a very different kind of workman, and which may well end in him being so different that he is expelled from his union. A Christian doctor will never regard a sick person as a case, but always as a person. A Christian employer will be concerned with far more than the mere payment of minimum wages or the creation of minimum working conditions. It is the simple fact of the matter that if enough Christians became *hagios*, different, answerable solely to Christ, they would revolutionize society. And that indeed, and in truth, is the Christian task. The word *blameless* is the Greek word *amōmos*. The interest of this word lies in the fact that it is a sacrificial word. Under Jewish law before an animal could be offered as a sacrifice it must be examined and inspected; and if any blemish was found it must be rejected as unfit for an offering to God. Only the best was fit to offer to God. This word *amōmos* thinks of the whole life and the whole man as an offering to God. It thinks of taking every part of our life, our work, our pleasure, our sport, our home life, our personal relationships, and making them all such that they can be taken and offered to God. This word does not mean that the Christian must be respectable; it means that he must be perfect. Simply to say that the Christian must be *amōmos* is to banish self-satisfaction, and to banish contentment with second bests; it is to challenge a man to make his whole life so perfect that it is a fit offering to God. It is the end of the spirit which says: " I know I have faults, but I can't change them "; it is the end of the spirit which knows that our work is not being done as well as it could be done, but which has become quite content with second bests. It simply means that the Christian standard is nothing less than perfection, and that the Christian sets no value on the judgments of human standards, but thinks only of how to satisfy the scrutiny of God.

THE PLAN OF GOD

Ephesians I: 5, 6

> He determined in His love before time began to adopt us to Himself through Jesus Christ, in the good purpose of His will, so that all might praise the glory of the generous gift which He freely gave us in the Beloved.

IN this passage Paul speaks to us of the plan of God. One of the pictures that Paul more than once uses of what God does for men is the picture of adoption (cf. *Romans* 8: 23; *Galatians* 4: 5). God adopted us as sons into His family. In the ancient world, where Roman law prevailed, this would be an even more meaningful picture than it is to us. In the Roman world the family was based on what was called the *patria potestas*, the father's power. Under Roman law a father had absolute power over his children so long as he and they lived. A Roman father could sell his child as a slave, and could even kill the child. According to ancient Roman law, and that law still operated in Paul's time, a father had the right of life and death over his children. Dion Cassius tells us that the Roman law was that "the law of the Romans gives a father absolute authority over his son, and that for the son's whole life. It gives him authority, if he so chooses, to imprison him, to scourge him, to make him work on his estate as a slave in fetters, even to kill him. That right still continues to exist even if the son is old enough to play an active part in political affairs, even if he has been judged worthy

91

to occupy the magistrate's office, and even if he is held in honour by all men." It is quite true that, when a father was judging his son, he was supposed to call the adult male members of the family into consultation, but it was not necessary that he should do so. There are actual instances of cases in which a father did condemn his son to death. Sallust (*The Catiline Conspiracy*, 39) tells how a son called Aulus Fulvius joined the rebel Catiline. He was arrested on the journey and brought back. And his father ordered that he should be put to death. The father did this on his own private authority. The father gave as his reason that " he had begotten him, not for Catiline against his country, but for his country against Catiline." Under Roman law a child could not possess anything; and any inheritance willed to him, or any gift given to him, became the property of his father. It did not matter how old the son was, or to what honours and responsibility he had risen, he was absolutely in his father's power. In circumstances like that it is obvious that adoption was a very serious step. It was a serious step to take a child out of one *patria potestas* and to put him into another. It was, however, not uncommon, for children were often adopted to ensure that some family should not become extinct, but should continue to exist. The ritual of adoption must have been very impressive. It was carried out by a symbolic sale in which copper and scales were used. Twice the real father sold his son, and twice he symbolically bought him back; finally he sold him a third time, and at the third sale he did not buy him back. After this the adopting father had to go to the *praetor*, one of the principal Roman magistrates, and plead the case for the adoption, and only after all this had been gone through was the adoption complete. But when the adoption was complete it was complete indeed. The person who had been adopted had all the rights of a legitimate son in his new family, and completely lost all rights in his old family. In the eyes of the law he was a new person. So new was he that even all debts and obligations connected with his previous family were cancelled out and abolished as if they had never existed.

That is what Paul says that God has done for us. We were absolutely in the power of sin and of the world; and God, through Jesus, took us out of that power into His power; and that adoption cancels and wipes out the past and we are made new. We have passed from the family of the world and of evil into the family of God.

THE GIFTS OF GOD

Ephesians I: 7, 8

> For it is in Him that we have a deliverance which cost His life; in Him we have received the forgiveness of sins, which only the wealth of His grace could give, a grace which He gave us in abundant supply, and which conferred on us all wisdom and all sound sense.

IN this short section we come face to face with three of the great conceptions of the Christian faith.

(i) There is the conception of *deliverance*. The word used is *apolutrōsis*. This word comes from the verb *lutroun*, which means *to ransom*. It is the word which is used for ransoming a man who is a prisoner of war or a slave. It is the word which is used for freeing a man from the penalty of death for some crime. It is the word used for God's deliverance of the children of Israel from their slavery in Egypt. It is the word used for God's continual rescuing of His people in the time of their trouble. In every case the conception is the delivering or the setting free of a man from a situation from which he himself was powerless to liberate himself, or from a penalty which he himself could never have paid. So, then, first of all Paul says that God delivered men from a situation from which they could never have delivered themselves. Now, in point of fact, that is precisely what Christianity did do for men. When Christianity came into this world men were haunted and oppressed by the sense of their own powerlessness. They knew their own sin and their own inadequacy; they knew the wrongness of the life which they were living; and they also knew that they were powerless to do anything about it. Seneca is full of this kind of feeling of sheer helpless frustration. Men, he said, were overwhelmingly conscious of their inefficiency in necessary things. He said of himself that he was a *homo non tolerabilis*, a man not to be tolerated. Men, he said with a kind of despair, love their vices and hate them at the same time. What men need, he cried, is a hand let down to lift them up. The highest thinkers, the sensitive minds in the pagan world knew that they were in the grip of something from which they were helpless to deliver themselves. They needed liberation; they needed some dynamic of power. And it was just that liberation which Jesus Christ brought. It is still true of Christ that by His power He can liberate men from this helpless slavery to the things which attract and disgust them at one and the same time. To put it at its simplest, Jesus can still make bad men good.

(ii) There is *forgiveness*. The ancient world was haunted by the sense of sin. It might well be said that the whole Old Testament is an expansion of the saying, " The soul that sinneth, it shall die " (*Ezekiel* 18: 4). Men were conscious of their own guilt and stood in terror of their god or gods. It is sometimes said that the Greeks had no sense of sin. Nothing could be further from the truth. " Men," said Hesiod, " delight their souls in cherishing that which is their bane." All the plays of Aeschylus are founded on one text—" The doer shall suffer." Once a man had done an evil thing Nemesis was on his heels; soon or late Nemesis would catch up on him; and punishment followed sin as certainly as night followed day. As Shakespeare had it in *Richard the Third*,

> " My conscience hath a thousand several tongues,
>   And every tongue brings in a several tale,
>   And every tale condemns me for a villain."

94

If there was one thing which men knew it was the sense of sin and the dread of God. Jesus changed all that. He opened the way to God. He taught men, not of the hate, but of the love of God. Because Jesus came into the world, men, even in their sin, discovered the love of God.

(iii) There is *wisdom* and *sound sense*. The two words in Greek are *sophia* and *phronēsis*, and Christ brought both of them to us. Now this is very interesting. The Greeks wrote and thought much about these two words; and if a man had both, that man would be perfectly equipped for life. Aristotle defined *sophia*, wisdom, as knowledge of the most precious things. Cicero defined it as knowledge of things both human and divine. *Sophia* was a thing of the searching intellect, of the questing mind, of the reaches of the thoughts of men. *Sophia* is the answer to the eternal problems of life and death, and God and man, and time and eternity. Aristotle defined *phronēsis* as the knowledge of human affairs, and of the things in which planning is necessary. Plutarch defined *phronēsis* as practical knowledge of the things which concern us. Cicero defined *phronēsis* as knowledge of the things which are to be sought and the things which are to be avoided. Plato defined *phronēsis* as the disposition of mind which enables us to judge what things are to be done and what things are not to be done. In other words, *phronēsis* is the most practical thing in the world. It is the sound sense which enables men to meet and to solve the practical problems of everyday life and living. It is Paul's claim that Jesus brought us *sophia*, knowledge of the eternal things, the intellectual knowledge which satisfies the mind; and that He brought us *phronēsis*, the practical knowledge which enables us to handle and to solve the day to day problems of practical life and living. There is a certain completeness in the Christian character. There is a type of person who is at home in the study, who moves familiarly amidst the theological and philosophical problems, and who is yet helpless and impractical in the ordinary everyday affairs of life. There is another kind of person who claims that he is a practical man, so engaged with the business of living that he has no time to concern himself with the ultimate things. In the light of the gifts of God through Christ, both of these characters are imperfect and one-sided. Christ brings to us the solution of the problems both of eternity and time. Christ gives to men the ability to see the great ultimate truths of eternity and to solve the problems of each moment of time.

THE GOAL OF HISTORY

Ephesians I: 9, 10

> This happened because He made known to us the once hidden but now revealed secret of His will, for so it was His good pleasure to do. The secret was a purpose which He formed in His own mind before time began, so that the periods of time should be controlled and administered until they reached their full development, a development in which all things, in heaven and upon earth, are gathered into one in Jesus Christ.

IT is now that Paul is really getting to grips with his subject. He says, as the Authorised Version has it, that now God has made known to us " the mystery of His will." The New Testament uses the word *mystery* in a special sense. In the New Testament sense a *mystery* is not some-thing mysterious in the sense that it is hard to understand. It is something which has long been kept secret, and which has now been revealed; and it is something which is still incomprehensible to the person who has not been initiated into its meaning. Let us take an example. Suppose someone who knew nothing whatever about Christianity was brought into a Communion Service. To him it would be a complete mystery; he would not understand in the least what was going on. But to a man who knows the story of Christ, to a man who knows the story and the meaning of the Last Supper, to a man who knows how Jesus left this memorial to His disciples, the whole service, and every action in it, has a meaning which is quite clear. So in the New Testament sense a mystery is something which is hidden to the heathen, but clear to the Christian. It is a secret the meaning of which has been revealed.

And what for Paul was the meaning of the mystery of the will of God? To Paul that mystery was that the gospel was open to the Gentiles too. Here was the great secret of God. Till Jesus came it had seemed that the Jews were God's chosen people; now God has revealed that His love and care, His grace and mercy, the good news of God, are meant, not only for the Jews, but for all the world.

And now Paul, in one sentence, drops his great thought. Up till now men had been living in a divided world. Wherever you look there is division. There was division between the beasts and men. Man's dominion had broken nature's social union. There was division between the Jew and the Gentile, the Greek and the barbarian. All over the world there was strife and tension, and war and hatred and separation. What was true of the world was true of the individual man. Every man is a walking civil war. Within him there is the tension, the division, the battle between right and wrong, between good and evil, between passion and reason, between the instincts and the will. Everywhere in this world there was division; and Jesus came into the world to wipe out the divisions, to resolve the tensions, to close the gaps and the separations, and to gather all men into one. That for Paul was the secret of God. It was God's purpose that all the many different strands, all the loose ends of things, all the warring, competing, hating elements in this world should be gathered into one unity and union in Jesus Christ. Jesus came to make the world into one world in Himself.

Now here we have another tremendous thought in Paul. Paul says that all history has been a working out of this process. He says that through all the ages there has been a planning, an arranging, and an administering of

97

things that this day of unity should come. The word which Paul uses for this preparation and planning is intensely interesting. It is the word *oikonomia*, which literally means *household management*. The *oikonomos* was the steward who saw to it that the family affairs ran smoothly and uninterruptedly. So Paul has the idea that all history has been a planning, and a thinking, and an administering and an arranging which would end in the world being one family in God.

It is the Christian conviction that history is a plan, that history has a purpose, that history is the working out of the will of God. That is by no means what every historian or thinker has been able to see. Oscar Wilde in one of his epigrams said: " You give the criminal calendar of Europe to your children under the name of history." G. N. Clark, in his inaugural lecture at Cambridge, said: " There is no secret and no plan in history to be discovered. I do not believe that any future consummation could make sense of all the irrationalities of preceding ages. If it could not explain them, still less could it justify them." In the introduction to *A History of Europe*, H. A. L. Fisher writes: " One intellectual excitement, however, has been denied to me. Men wiser and more learned than I have discovered in history a plot, a rhythm, a predetermined pattern. These harmonies are concealed from me. I can see only one emergency following another, as wave follows upon wave, only one great fact with respect to which, since it is unique, there can be no generalizations, only one safe rule for the historian: that he should recognize in the development of human destinies the play of the contingent and the unforeseen." Andre Maurois says: " The universe is indifferent. Who created it? Why are we here on this puny mud-heap spinning in infinite space? I have not the slightest idea, and I am quite convinced that no one has the least idea." It so happens that we are living in an age in which men have lost their faith in any purpose for this world. But it is the faith of the Christian that in this world God's purpose is being worked out; and it is the conviction of Paul that that purpose is that one day all things, and all men, should be one family in Christ. To that, as Paul sees it, all history has been moving. As Paul sees it, that secret, that mystery was not even grasped until Jesus came. As Paul sees it, it is the great task of the Church to work out that purpose of unity, which is the purpose of God, revealed in Jesus Christ.

JEW AND GENTILE

Ephesians I: 11-14

It was in Christ, in whom our portion in this scheme was also assigned to us, that it was determined, by the decision of Him who controls everything according to the purpose of His good will, that we, who were the first to set our hopes upon the coming of the Anointed One of God, should become the means whereby His glory should be praised. And it was in Christ that it was determined that you too should become the means whereby God's glory is praised, after you had heard the word which brings the truth, the good news of your salvation—that good news in which after you had believed you were sealed with the Holy Spirit, who had been promised to you, the Spirit who is the foretaste and guarantee of all that one day we will inherit, until we enter into that complete redemption which brings complete possession.

HERE is Paul's first example of the new unity which Christ brings. When Paul speaks of *us* he means his own nation, the Jews; when he speaks of *you* he means the Gentiles to whom he is writing; and when in the very last sentence he again uses the word *us*, it is of Jews and Gentiles together that he is thinking.

First of all, then, Paul speaks of the Jews. They, too, had their portion assigned to them in the plan of God. They were the first to believe in, and to expect, the coming of the Anointed One of God. All through their history the Jews had hoped for, and dreamed of, and expected the Messiah. Their part in the scheme of things was to be the nation from whom God's chosen one should come. Adam Smith, the great economist, argued that the whole pattern of life was founded on what he called *the division of labour*. He meant that life can only go on when each man has a job and does that job, and when the results of all the jobs are pooled and become the common stock. The shoemaker makes shoes; the baker makes bread; the tailor makes clothes; each has his own job, and each sticks to his own job; and when each efficiently carries out his job the total good of the whole community follows. What is true of individuals is true also of nations. Each nation has its place and its part in God's scheme of things. The Greeks taught men what beauty of thought and form is. The Romans taught men law and the science of government and administration. The Jews taught men religion. The Jews were the people who were so prepared that from them God's Messiah should come. That is not to say that God did not prepare other people too. If there had been no preparation of other nations then when the message of Christianity went out the world would have been unable to receive it. All over the world God had been preparing men and nations so that their mind would be ready to receive the message when it came. But the great privilege of the Jewish nation was that they were the first nation to expect and to await the coming of the Anointed One of God into the world.

Then Paul turns to the Gentiles. In their development Paul sees three stages. (i) They received the word. To them the Christian preachers brought the Christian message. That word which they received was two things. First, it was the word of truth. It brought them the truth about God, and the truth about the world in which they lived, and the truth about themselves. Second, it was good news. Christianity is characteristically good news about God. It is the message of the love and of the grace of God. (ii) They were sealed with the Holy Spirit. In the ancient world—and it is a custom which is still followed —when a sack, or a crate, or a package was despatched, it was sealed with a seal, in order to guarantee that it came from the sender, and that it was intact. The seal indicated from where the package had come and to whom it belonged. The possession of the Holy Spirit is the seal and sign which shows that a man belongs to God. It is the Holy Spirit who brings a man the knowledge of God; it is the Holy Spirit who enables a man to cope with life and not to collapse; it is the Holy Spirit who tells a man what to do and who gives him strength to do it. The Holy Spirit both shows us God's will and enables us to do it.

Now here Paul says a very great thing about the Holy Spirit. He calls the Holy Spirit, as the Authorized Version has it, *the earnest of our redemption*. The Greek word is *arrabōn*. The *arrabōn* was a regular feature of the Greek business world. The *arrabōn* was a part of the purchase price of anything paid in advance as a guarantee that the rest of the price would in due time be paid. There are many Greek commercial documents still extant in which the word occurs. A woman sells a cow and she receives so many drachmae as *arrabōn*, that is, as guarantee and surety that the full purchase price will duly be paid. Some dancing girls are engaged for a public entertainment; and they are paid so much in advance as a guarantee that the remainder of the money will be paid, and the contract will be honoured, after the performance has been given. So what Paul is saying is that the experience of the Holy Spirit which we have in this world is a foretaste of the joys and of the blessedness of heaven; and it is the guarantee that some day we will enter into the fullness of knowledge, of power and of joy. It is the guarantee that some day we will enter into full possession of the bliss and the blessedness of God.

Here is the great truth that the greatest and the highest, and the dearest and the most intimate experience of Christian peace and joy which this world can afford, are only faint foretastes of the joy into which we will one day enter. It is as if God had given us enough to whet our appetites for more, and enough to make us certain that some day He will give us all.

THE MARKS OF THE CHURCH

Ephesians I: 15-23

It is because I have heard of your faith in Jesus Christ, and your love to all God's consecrated people, that I never cease to give thanks for you, as I remember you in my prayers. It is the aim of my prayers that the God of our Lord Jesus Christ, the glorious Father, may give you the Spirit of wisdom, the Spirit which brings you new revelation, as you come to know Him more and more fully. It is the aim of my prayers that the eyes of your heart may be enlightened, so that you may know what hope His calling has brought to you, what wealth of glory there is in our inheritance among the saints, what surpassing greatness there is in His power to us who believe with a belief which was wrought by the might of His strength, that power which wrought in Christ to raise Him from among the dead, and to set Him at God's right hand in the heavenly places, above every rule and authority and power and lordship, above every dignity which is held in honour, not only in this age, but also in the age to come. God subjected all things to Him, and He gave Him as head above all to the Church, which is His body, the Church which is His complement on earth, the Church which belongs to Him who is filling all things in all places.

THE supremely important part, the second great step in Paul's argument, lies at the very end of this passage; but before we reach it there are certain things we must note in the verses which go before.

Here there is set out before us in a perfect summary the characteristics of a true Church. Paul has heard of their faith in Christ and their love to all God's consecrated people. The two things which must characterize any true Church are *loyalty to Christ* and *love to men*. There is a loyalty to Christ which does not issue in love to men. The monks and the hermits had a loyalty to Christ which separated them from their fellow men, and which made them abandon the ordinary activities of life in order to live alone in the desert places. The heresy hunters of the Spanish Inquisition and of many another age had a loyalty to Christ which made them persecute those who thought differently from them. Before Jesus came the Pharisees had a loyalty to God which made them self-righteous and contemptuous of those whom they thought less loyal than themselves. The true Christian loves Christ, and loves his fellow men. More than that, the true Christian knows that he cannot show his love to Christ in any other way than by showing his love to his fellow men. However orthodox a Church is, however pure its theology, and however noble its worship and its liturgy, it is not a true Church in the real sense of the term unless it is characterized by love for its fellow men. There are Churches which seldom make any public pronouncement which is not based on censorious criticism, and the accent of whose voice is continuous criticism. They may be orthodox, but they are not Christian. The true Church is marked by a double love—love for Christ and love for men. F. W. Boreham quotes a passage from Robert Buchanan's *Shadow of the Sword*, in which Buchanan describes the Chapel of Hate. " It stood on a bleak and barren moor in Brittany a hundred years ago. It was in ruins; the walls were black and stained with the slime of centuries; around the crumbling altar nettles and rank weeds grew breast high; whilst black mists, charged with rain, brooded night and day about the gloomy scene. Over the doorway of the chapel, but half-obliterated, was its name. It was dedicated to Our Lady of Hate. ' Hither,' says Buchanan, ' in hours of passion and pain, came men and women to cry curses on their enemies—the maiden on her false lover, the lover on his false mistress, the husband on his false wife—praying, one and all, that Our Lady of Hate might hearken, and that the hated one might die within the year.' " And then the novelist adds: " So bright and so deep had the gentle Christian light shone within their minds! " A chapel of hate is a grim conception; and yet—are we always so very far away from it? We hate the liberals or the radicals; we hate the fundamentalists or the obscurantists; we hate the man whose theology is different from our own; we hate the Roman Catholic or the Protestant as the case may be. We make pronouncements which are characterized, not by Christian charity, but by a kind of condemning bitterness. We would do well to remember every now and then that love of Christ and love of our fellow men cannot exist without each other. Our tragedy is that it is so often true, as Swift once said: " We have just enough religion to make us hate, but not enough to make us love one another."

PAUL'S PRAYER FOR THE CHURCH

Ephesians I: 15-23 (*continued*)

HERE in this passage we see what Paul prays for for a Church which he loves and a Church which is doing well.

(i) He prays for the Spirit of Wisdom. The word that he uses for *wisdom* is *sophia,* and we have already seen that *sophia* is the word for wisdom of the deep things of God. He prays that the Church may be led deeper and deeper into the knowledge of the eternal truths. If ever that is to happen in the Church, certain things are necessary. (*a*) It is necessary that we should have a thinking people. Boswell tells us that Goldsmith once said: " As I take my shoes from the shoemaker, and my coat from the tailor, so I take my religion from the priest." There are many who are like that; and yet religion is nothing unless it is a personal discovery. As Plato had it long ago: " The unexamined life is the life not worth living," and the unexamined religion is the religion not worth having. It is an obligation for a thinking man to think his way to God. (*b*) It is necessary that we should have a teaching ministry. William Chillingworth said: "The Bible, and the Bible only, is the religion of Protestants." That is true; but so often we would not think so. The exposition of scripture from the pulpit is a first necessity of religious wakening. We are interested, not in what a preacher thinks, but in what God says. (*c*) It is necessary that we should have a readjusted sense of proportion. It is one of the strange facts of Church life that in Church courts, such as sessions and presbyteries, and even General Assemblies, a score of hours is given to the discussion of mundane problems of administration for every one that is given to the discussion of the eternal verities of God. It is in fact true that a theological discussion of any kind in a court of the Church is nowadays a rarity. Paul prayed that his people might be led into a deeper wisdom of the eternal things. That prayer can never be answered if we never allot any time to thinking about them.

(ii) Paul prays for a fuller revelation and a fuller knowledge of God. For the Christian growth in knowledge and in grace is essential. Any man who follows any profession knows that he dare not stop studying. No doctor thinks that he has finished learning when he leaves the classrooms of his university. He knows that week by week, and almost day by day, new techniques and drugs and treatments are being discovered; and if he wishes to retain his skill as a doctor, and to continue to be of service to those in illness and in pain, he must keep up with them. It is so with the Christian. The Christian life could be described as getting to know God better every day. A friendship which does not grow closer with the years tends to vanish with the years. And it is so with us and God.

(iii) He prays for a new realization of the Christian hope. It is almost a characteristic of the age in which we live that it is an age of despair. Thomas Hardy wrote in Tess: " Sometimes I think that the worlds are like apples on our stubbard tree. Some of them splendid and some of them blighted." Then comes the question: " On which kind do we live—a splendid one or a blighted one? " And Tess's answer is: " A blighted one." Between the wars Sir Philip Gibbs wrote: " If I smell poison gas in Edgeware Road, I am not going to put on a gas mask or go to a gas-proof room. I am going out to take a good sniff of it, for I shall know that *the game is up.*" Men feel that they are living in a world where the game is up. H. G. Wells once wrote grimly: " Man, who began in a cave behind a windbreak, will end in the disease-soaked ruins of a slum." On every side the voice of the pessimist sounds; there never was a time when it was more necessary to sound the trumpet-call of Christian hope. If the Christian message is true, and if God is as Jesus Christ taught us that He is, then the world is not on the way to dissolution but to consummation.

(iv) He prays for a new realization of the power of God. For Paul the supreme proof of the power of God was the Resurrection. When sin had done everything in its power to destroy Christ, when men had gone to the limit of human action to eliminate Christ, the Resurrection of Jesus was the proof that God's power is stronger than man's sin, and that God's purpose cannot be stopped by any action of men. In a world which looks like a chaotic world it is well to remember that the unknown steersman whom men call God is still in control.

(v) Paul finishes by speaking of the conquest of Christ in a sphere which does not mean so much to us to-day. As the Authorized Version has it, God has raised Jesus Christ " far above all principality, and power, and might, and dominion, and every name that is named." In the days of Paul men strongly believed both in demons and in angels; and these words which Paul uses are the titles of different grades of angels. What Paul is saying is that there is not a being in heaven or on earth to whom Jesus Christ is not superior and than whom He is not greater

It is as if Paul said: " In Jesus you have the greatest and most powerful friend and saviour in heaven and on earth." In essence Paul's prayer is that men should realize the greatness of the Lord and Saviour God has given to them.

THE BODY OF CHRIST

Ephesians I: 15-23 (continued)

So now we come to the last two verses of this chapter, and in them Paul has one of the greatest, and most adventurous, and most uplifting thoughts that any man has ever had. In these verses he calls the Church by its greatest title—*the body of Christ*. Christ is the head of the Church, and the Church is the body of Christ.

In order to understand what Paul means, let us go back to the basic thought of this whole letter. As it stands, this world is a complete disunity. There is disunity between Jew and Gentile, between Greek and barbarian; there is disunity between different men within the same nation; there is disunity within every man, for in every man the good strives with the evil; there is disunity between man and the beasts, so that man and the beasts are enemies instead of friends; and, above all, there is disunity between man and God. It was Paul's thesis that Jesus died to bring all the discordant elements in this universe into one, to wipe out the breaches and the separations, to reconcile man to man and to reconcile man to God. Jesus Christ was above all things God's instrument of reconciliation.

It was to bring all things and all men into one family and one unity that Christ died. But, clearly, that unity does not as yet exist. Now let us take a human analogy. Suppose a great doctor, working in his laboratory and in his hospital wards, discovers a cure for cancer, once that cure is found it is there. But before it can become available for everyone, and before the sufferers from cancer all over the world can be cured, that cure must be taken out to the world. Doctors and surgeons must know about it, and must be trained to use it. The cure is there; but the one man cannot take it out to all the world; a corps of doctors must learn about it and about how to handle it, and they must be the agents whereby the cure arrives at all the world's sufferers. That precisely is what the Church is to Jesus Christ. It is in Jesus that all men and all nations can become one. But before that can happen all men and all nations must know about Jesus Christ. His truth, His grace, His forgiveness, His love must be brought to all men. And that is the task of the Church. Jesus Christ is God's instrument whereby the discordant elements in the warring world can be brought into one with each other and one with God; and the Church is the instrument of Jesus Christ whereby that unity can be carried out.

Christ is the head; the Church is the body. A head by itself is no use; a mind, a brain by itself is of no use. The head must have a body which it can direct; the brain, the mind must have a body through which it can work. The Church is quite literally hands to do Christ's work, feet to run upon His errands, a voice to speak His words.

In the very last phrase of the chapter Paul has two tremendous thoughts. The Church, he says, is the comple-ment of Christ. Just as the body is the complement of the brain, the Church is the complement of Christ. Just as the ideas and the thoughts and the discoveries of the mind cannot become effective without the work of the body, the tremendous secret and glory which Christ brought to this world cannot be made effective without the work of the Church. Then Paul goes on to say that Jesus is bit by bit filling all things in all places; and that filling is being wrought out by the Church. Into all lands and to all men the Church must bring the secret of Jesus

Christ. This is one of the most tremendous thoughts in all Christianity. It means nothing less than that God's plan for one world is in the hands of the Church. It was God's purpose to make a world where all the warring elements were welded into one with each other, and one with Him. To make that plan possible He sent Jesus Christ. In Jesus is the secret of unity. But the message and the power must be taken out to all men; and the Church is the body of Christ, the instrument through which Christ acts throughout the world. It is on the Church that the fulfilment of God's plan depends.

There is an illustration which is old and hackneyed, but which perfectly sums up this great truth. There is a legend which tells how Jesus went back to heaven after His time on earth. Even in heaven He bore upon Him the marks of the suffering and the Cross. The angels were talking to Him, and Gabriel said: " Master, you must have suffered terribly for men down there." " I did," said Jesus. " And," said Gabriel, " do they all know about how you loved them and what you did for them?' " O no," said Jesus, " not yet. Just now only a few people in Palestine know." " What have you done," said Gabriel, " to let everyone know about it? " Jesus said: " I have asked Peter and James and John and a few others to make it the business of their lives to tell others about me, and the others still others, and yet others, until the farthest man on the widest circle knows about what I have done." Gabriel looked very doubtful, for Gabriel knew well what poor stuff men were made off. " Yes," he said, " but what if Peter and James and John grow tired? What if the people who come after them forget? What if away down in the twentieth century people just don't tell others about you? Haven't you made any other plans? " And Jesus answered: " I haven't made any other plans. *I'm counting on them.*" To say that the Church is the Body, the complement of Christ exactly means that Jesus is counting on us.

THE CHRISTLESS LIFE AND THE GRACE OF GOD

EPHESIANS 2: 1-10

WHEN you were dead in your sins and trespasses, those sins and trespasses in which once you walked, living life in the way in which this present age of this world lives it, living life as the ruler of the power of the air dictates it, that spirit who now operates in the children of disobedience— and once all we too lived the same kind of life as these children of disobedience do, a life in which we were at the mercy of the desires of our lower nature, a life in which we followed the wishes of our lower nature and of our own designs, a life in which, so far as human nature goes, we deserved nothing but the wrath of God, as the others do— although we were all like that, I say, God, because He is rich in mercy, and because of His great love with which He has loved us, made us alive in Christ Jesus, even when we were dead in trespasses (it is by grace you have been saved), and raised us up with Christ, and gave us a seat in the heavenly places with Christ, because of what Christ Jesus did for us. This He did so that in the age to come the surpassing riches of His grace in His kindness to us in Christ Jesus might be demonstrated. For it is by grace appropriated by faith that you have been saved. You had nothing to do with this. It was God's gift to you. It was not the result of works, for it was God's design that no one should be able to boast. For we are His work, created in Christ Jesus for good works, works which God prepared beforehand that we might walk in them.

IN this passage Paul's thought flows on regardless of the rules of grammar; he begins sentences, and never finishes them; he begins with one construction, and halfway through he glides into another, and forgets the first. That is so because this is far more a lyric of the love of God than a careful theological exposition. The song of the nightingale is not to be analysed by the laws of counterpoint and musical composition. The lark sings for the joy of singing. That is what Paul is doing here. He is pouring out his heart, and the claims of grammar have to give way to the wonder of grace.

LIFE WITHOUT CHRIST

Ephesians 2: 1-3

> When you were dead in your sins and trespasses, those
> sins and trespasses in which you once walked, living
> life in the way this present age lives it, living life as the
> ruler of the power of the air dictates it, that spirit
> who now operates in the children of disobedience—and
> once all we too lived the same kind of life as these
> children of disobedience do, a life in which we were
> at the mercy of the desires of our lower nature, a life
> in which we followed the wishes of our lower nature
> and of our own designs, a life in which, as far as
> human nature goes, we deserved nothing but the wrath
> of God, as the others do.

WHEN Paul speaks of *you*, he is speaking of the Gentiles;
when he speaks of *us* he is speaking of the Jews, his own
fellow countrymen. In this passage he shows how terrible
the Christless life was for Gentile and for Jew alike.

(i) First of all, he says that that life was lived in sins
and trespasses. The words he uses are very interesting.
The word for *sin* is *hamartia*; and *hamartia* is a shooting
word. It literally means a *miss*. A man shoots his arrow
at the target; the arrow misses; that is *hamartia*. This
shows us that sin is the failure to hit the target of life;
sin is the failure to be what we ought to be and what we
could be. That is precisely why sin is so universal. We
commonly have a wrong idea of sin. We would readily
agree that the robber, the murderer, the razor-slasher, the
drunkard, the gangster are sinners; but, since most of
us are respectable citizens, in our heart of hearts we think
that sin has not very much to do with us. We would
probably rather resent being called hell-deserving sinners.
But this word *hamartia* brings us face to face with what
sin is. Sin, let us repeat it, is the failure to be what we
ought to be and could be. Is a man as good a husband
as he might be? Does he try to make life easier for his wife?
Does he inflict his moods and temperaments and irritabilities
on his family? Is a woman as good a wife as she might be?

K—5   III

Does she really take an interest in her husband's work and try to understand the problems and the worries of a man on whose work the home depends? Are we as good parents as we might have been? Have we really disciplined and trained our children as we ought, or have we often shirked the issue? As our children grew older, have we come nearer and nearer to them, or have they drifted away until conversation is often difficult, and we and they are practically strangers? Are we as good sons and daughters as we might have been? Have we ever even tried to say thank you for, or to repay what has been done for us? Have we ever seen the hurt look in our parents' eyes and known that we put it there? Have we been as good workmen as we could have been? Is every working hour filled with our hardest and our most conscientious work, and is every task done as well as we could possibly do it? When we realize what sin is, we come to see that sin is not something which theologians have invented. It is something with which life is soaked and saturated and permeated. Sin is the failure in any sphere of life to be what we ought to be and could be. The other word that Paul uses is translated *trespasses*, and is the word *paraptōma*. This is a word which literally means *a slip* or *a fall*. It is used for a man losing the way, and straying from the right road; it is used for a man failing to grasp, and slipping away from the truth. Sin, trespass, is taking the wrong road, when we could have and should have taken the right one; it is missing the truth that we might have known and should have known; and therefore sin is the failure to reach the goal and journey's end we ought to have reached. Are we in life where we ought to be? Have we reached the goal of efficiency, skill, talent, craftsmanship that our gifts might have enabled us to reach? Have we reached the goal of service to others that we might have reached? Have we reached the goal of goodness to which we might have attained? Are we on the right road, or did we lose it, and drift away from it somewhere back along the road?

The great central idea of sin is failure, failure to hit the target, failure to hold to the road, failure to make life what life was capable of becoming; and that definition of sin includes every one of us. When we understand what sin is, we are left in no doubt as to the universality of sin, and in no possible doubt of our own sin.

DEATH IN LIFE

Ephesians 2: 1-3 (continued)

PAUL speaks about people being *dead in sins*. What did he mean by that phrase? Some have taken it to mean that without Christ men live in a state of sin which in the life to come produces the death of the soul. But Paul is not talking about the life to come; he is talking about this present life in this world. Sin always has a killing power. There are three directions in which the effect of sin is fatal and deadly.

(i) *Sin kills innocence.* No one is precisely the same after he has sinned. The psychologists tell us that quite literally we never forget anything. A thing may not be in our conscious memory and on the surface of the things which we remember, but everything we ever did or saw or heard is buried in our subconscious memories. We may not know that we remember it, but it is there. The result of that is that sin leaves a permanent effect on a man. In Du Maurier's novel *Trilby* there is an example of that. For the first time in his life Little Billee has taken part in a drunken debauch and has himself been drunk. " And when, after some forty-eight hours or so, he had quite slept off the fumes of that memorable Christmas debauch, he found that a sad thing had happened to him, and a strange ! It is as though a tarnishing breath had swept over the reminiscent mirror of his mind and left a little film behind it, so that no past thing he wished to see therein was reflected with quite the same pristine clearness. As though the keen, quick, razor edge of his power to reach and re-evoke the by-gone charm and glamour and essence of things had been blunted and coarsened. As though the bloom of that special joy, the gift he had of recalling past emotions and sensations and situations, and making them actual once more by a mere effort of will, had been brushed away. And he never recovered the full use of that most precious faculty, the boon of youth and happy childhood, and which he had once possessed, without knowing it, in such singular and exceptional completeness." The experience of sin had left a kind of tarnishing film on his mind and on his memory, and things could never be quite the same again. If we stain a garment or a carpet, we may send it to the cleaners to be cleaned, but it is never again quite the same. Sin does something to a man; it kills innocence; and innocence, once lost, can never be recovered.

(ii) *Sin kills ideals.* In the lives of so many there is a kind of tragic process. At first a man regards some wrong thing with horror; the second stage comes when he is tempted into doing it, but even as he does it, he is still unhappy and ill at ease and very conscious that it is wrong; the third stage is when he has done the thing so often that he does it without a qualm. The fatal power of sin is that each sin makes the next sin easier; each indulgence makes the next indulgence easier. Wordsworth in the *Intimations of Immortality* wrote:

" The youth, who daily from the east
Must travel, still is Nature's priest,
    And by the vision splendid
    Is on his way attended;
At length the man perceives it die away,
And fade into the light of common day."

The ideal slowly dies, and every sin, every failure, every self-indulgence helps it to die. Sin is a kind of suicide, for sin kills the ideals which make life worth while.

(iii) In the end *sin kills the will.* At first a man engages in some forbidden pleasure because he wants to do so; in the end he engages in it because he cannot help doing so. Once a thing becomes a habit it is not far from being a necessity. When a man has allowed some habit, some indulgence, some secret or forbidden practice to master him, he becomes its slave. His will is helpless; its power is dead. As the old saying has it, " Sow an act and reap a habit; sow a habit and reap a character; sow a character and reap a destiny."

There is a certain murderous power in sin. Sin kills innocence; sin may be forgiven but the effect of sin remains. As Origen had it: " The scars remain." Sin kills ideals; men begin to do without a qualm the thing which once they regarded with horror. Sin kills the will; the thing so grips a man that he cannot break its grip.

All that is at least part of what Paul meant when he spoke of being dead in sin.

THE MARKS OF THE CHRISTLESS LIFE

Ephesians 2: 1-3 (*continued*)

IN this passage Paul makes a kind of list of the characteristics of life without Christ.

(i) It is life lived in the way this present age of this world lives it. That is to say, it is life lived on the world's standards and with the world's values. Christianity demands *forgiveness*, but the ancient writers said that it was a sign of weakness to have the power to avenge oneself for injury and not to do so. Christianity demands *love* even to our enemies, but Plutarch said that the sign of a good man was that he was useful to his friends and terrible to his enemies. Christianity demands *service*, but the world cannot understand the missionary, for instance, who goes away to some foreign land to teach in a school or heal in a hospital for a quarter of the salary he or she might obtain at home in some secular service. The essence of the world's standard is that it sets self in the centre;

the essence of the Christian standard is that it sets Christ and others in the centre. The essence of the worldly man is, as someone has said, that " he knows the price of everything and the value of nothing." The world's motive is the profit motive; the Christian's dynamic is the desire to serve.

(ii) It is life lived under the dictates of the prince of the air. Here again we are at something which was very real in the days of Paul, but which is not so real to us to-day. The ancient world believed strenuously in demons. They believed that the air was so crowded with these demons that there was not room to insert a pinpoint between them. Pythagoras said: " The whole air is full of spirits." Philo said: " There are spirits flying everywhere through the air." " The air is the house of the disembodied spirits." These demons were not all bad, but many of them were. They were out to propagate evil and to frustrate the purposes of God and to seduce men into their own evil ways. They were out to ruin the souls of men. The man who is under their domination is the man who has taken his side against God.

(iii) It is a life which is characterized by disobedience. God has many ways of revealing His will to men. He does so by conscience, the voice of the Holy Spirit speaking within us; He does so by giving to men the wisdom and the commandments of His book; He does so through the advice and the warning and the rebuke of good and godly men. But the man who lives the Christless life takes his own way of things, even when he knows what God's way is.

(iv) It is a life which is at the mercy of desire. The word for desire is *epithumia*, and *epithumia* characteristically means the desire for the wrong and the forbidden thing. To succumb to that desire is inevitably to come to disaster. One of the tragedies of the nineteenth century was the career of Oscar Wilde. He had a brilliant mind, and won the highest academic honours; he was a scintillating writer, and won the highest rewards in literature;

he had all the charm in the world, and he was a man whose instinct it was to be kind; yet he fell to the temptation of unnatural vice, and came to prison and disgrace. When he was suffering for his fall he wrote his book *De Profundis* and in it he said: " The gods had given me almost everything. But I let myself be lured into long spells of senseless and sensual ease. . . . Tired of being on the heights I deliberately went to the depths in search for new sensation. What the paradox was to me in the sphere of thought, perversity became to me in the sphere of passion. I grew careless of the lives of others. I took pleasure where it pleased me, and passed on. I forgot that every little action of the common day makes or unmakes character, and that therefore what one has done in the secret chamber, one has some day to cry aloud from the house-top. I ceased to be lord over myself. I was no longer the captain of my soul, and did not know it. I allowed pleasure to dominate me. I ended in horrible disgrace." Desire is a bad master, and to be at the mercy of desire is to be a slave. And desire is not simply a fleshly thing; it is the desire for any forbidden thing.

(v) It is the life which follows what the Authorized Version calls the desires of our flesh. Now we must be careful to understand what Paul means by the flesh and the sins of the flesh. He means far more than fleshly and bodily and sexual sins. In *Galatians* 5: 19-21 Paul lists the sins of the flesh. True, he starts with adultery and fornication, but he goes on to list idolatry, hatred, wrath, strife, envyings, seditions, heresies. The flesh is the lower part of our nature; the flesh is that part of our nature which gives sin a bridgehead and a point of attack. The meaning of the flesh will vary from person to person. One man's weakness may be in his body and his risk may be sexual sin; another man's sin may be in spiritual things and his risk may be in pride; another man's sin may be in earthly things and his risk may be unworthy ambition; another man's sin may be in his temper and his risk may be in envyings and strife. All are sins of the flesh. Let no man think that, because he has escaped the grosser sins of the body, he has avoided the sins of the flesh; and let no man think, because his body is hard to control, that he is the only one who is fighting with the sins of the flesh. The flesh is anything in us which gives sin its chance; it is human nature without God. To live according to the dictates of the flesh is simply to live in such a way that our lower nature, the worse part of us, dominates our lives.

(vi) It is life which is deserving only of the wrath of God. There is many a man whose life is embittered because he feels that in this life he has never had what his talents and his gifts and his work deserve; that may be so; but in the sight of God there is no man who deserves anything but condemnation. If God treated us as we deserve, there would be nothing but condemnation and punishment for the best of us. It is only His love in Christ which has forgiven the men who deserved nothing but punishment from Him, men who had grieved His love and broken His law.

THE WORK OF CHRIST
Ephesians 2: 4-10

Although we were all like that, I say, God, because He is rich in mercy, and because of His great love with which He has loved us, made us alive in Jesus Christ, even when we were dead in trespasses (it is by grace you have been saved), and raised us up with Christ, and gave us a seat in the heavenly places with Christ, because of what Christ Jesus did for us. This He did so that in the age to come the surpassing riches of His grace in His kindness to us in Christ Jesus might be demonstrated. For it is by grace appropriated by faith that you have been saved. You had nothing to do with this. It was God's gift to you. It was not the result of works, for it was God's design that no one should be able to boast. For we are His work, created in Christ Jesus for good works,

works which God prepared beforehand that we might walk in them.

PAUL had begun by saying that, as we are, we are dead in sins and trespasses; now he says that God in His love and mercy has made us alive in Jesus Christ. What exactly did he mean by that? Through what Jesus did something happened to reverse the process of life. We saw that there were three things involved in being dead in sins and trespasses. Jesus has something to do about each of these three things.

(i) We saw that sin kills innocence. Now not even Jesus can give a man back his lost innocence, for not even Jesus can put the clock back; but what Jesus can do is to take away the sense of guilt which the lost innocence necessarily brings with it. The first thing that sin always does is to create the feeling of estrangement between us and God. Whenever a man realizes that he has sinned, he is oppressed with the feeling that he dare not approach God. When Isaiah received the vision of God, his first reaction was to say: " Woe is me! for I am undone; because I am a man of unclean lips, and I dwell in the midst of a people of unclean lips " (*Isaiah* 6: 5). When Peter realized who Jesus was, his first reaction was: " Depart from me, for I am a sinful man, O Lord " (*Luke* 5: 8). Jesus begins by taking that sense of estrangement away. He came to tell us that no matter what we are like the door is open to us to the presence of God. Suppose there was a son or daughter who did some utterly shameful thing, and who then ran away, because he or she was sure that there was no use in going home, because the door was bound to be shut. Then suppose someone came with the news that, so far from being shut, the door was still open and a welcome was waiting at home. What a difference that news would make! It was just that news that Jesus brought. He came to take the sense of estrangement and of guilt away, by telling us that God wants us just as we are.

(ii) We saw that sin killed the ideals by which men live. Jesus reawakens the ideal in the heart of man. The story is told of a negro engineer in a river ferry-boat in America. His boat was old and he did not worry over much about it, and the engines were soiled and begrimed and ill-cared for. This engineer was soundly converted. The first thing he did was to go back to his ferry-boat and polish his engines until every part of the machinery shone like a mirror. One of the regular passengers commented on the change. " What have you been up to? " he asked the engineer. " What set you cleaning and polishing these old engines of yours? " " Sir," answered the engineer, " I've got a glory." That is what Christ does for a man. He gives a man a glory. It is told that in the congregation in Edinburgh to which George Matheson came there was an old woman who lived in a cellar in filthy conditions. After some months of Matheson's ministry, communion time came round. When the elder called at this old woman's cellar with the cards, he found that she had gone. He tracked her down. He found her in an attic room. She was very poor and there were no luxuries, but the attic was as light and airy and clean as the cellar had been dark and dismal and dirty. " I see you've changed your house," he said to her. " Ay," she said, " I have. You canna hear George Matheson preach and live in a cellar." The Christian message had rekindled the ideal. As the old hymn has it:

> " Deep in the human heart, crushed by the tempter,
> Feelings lie buried that grace can restore."

The grace of Jesus Christ rekindles the ideals which repeated falling to sin had extinguished. And by that very rekindling, life is set climbing again.

(iii) But, greater than anything else, Jesus Christ revives and restores and recreates the lost will. We saw that the fatal and the deadly thing about sin was that it slowly but surely destroyed a man's will, that the indulgence which had begun as a pleasure became a necessity, that a man's sins sapped his strength of will and forged chains by which a man was helplessly bound. Jesus recreates the will. That in fact is always what love does. The effect of a great love is always a cleansing thing. When a person really and truly falls in love, there enters into his life a greater love than the love of his sins. The new love compels him to goodness. He loves the loved one so much that the love of his sins is defeated and broken. That is what Christ does for us. When we love Him, that very love recreates and restores our will towards goodness. As the hymn has it:

" He breaks the power of cancelled sin,
He sets the prisoner free."

THE WORK AND THE WORKS OF GRACE

Ephesians 2: 4-10 *(continued)*

PAUL closes this passage with one of the great expositions of the paradox which always lies at the heart of the Pauline view of the gospel. Let us look at the two arms of that paradox.

(i) Paul insists that it is by grace that we are saved. We have nothing to do with our own salvation. We have not earned it, and we could never have earned it. It is the gift of God, and all that we can do is to accept it in the faith that this free offer of God is true. In this Paul's point of view is undeniably and unarguably true. And it is true for two reasons. (*a*) God is perfection, and nothing that we could ever bring would in any event satisfy the perfection of God. Nothing that finite, sinning man can do can ever earn or win or merit or deserve the approval and the favour of the infinite God of infinite goodness. Only perfection is good enough for God, and man by his very nature cannot bring perfection to God. Even if man was not a sinner, if ever man is to win his way to God, it must always be God who gives and man who takes. (*b*) But there is more than that. It is the great Christian conception that God is love. Sin is therefore a crime, not against law, but against love. Now it is possible to make atonement for a broken law, but it is impossible to make atonement for a broken heart; and sin is not so much breaking God's law as it is breaking God's heart. Suppose we break some law, we can pay the penalty, either of fine or of imprisonment which the law lays down, and then the law has no further claim on us; we are free of the law. But suppose we break someone's heart, we can never atone for that. Let us take a crude and imperfect analogy. Suppose a motorist by careless driving runs over and kills a child He will be arrested; he will be tried; he will be found guilty; he will be sentenced to such and such a term of imprisonment, or to such and such a fine; and his licence may be taken from him for such and such a period. But after he has paid the fine and served the imprisonment's term, the law has no further claim on him. As far as the law is concerned, the whole matter is over. But it is very different in relation to the mother whose child he killed. He can never make things up to her, he can never put things right with her, by serving a term of imprisonment or by paying a fine. It is against her love for her child that he has committed this crime; and the only thing which can restore his relationship to her is an act of free forgiveness on her part. That is the way we are to God. It is not God's laws against which we have sinned; it is against God's heart. And therefore only an act of free forgiveness of the grace of God can put us back into the right relationship with God. We can never earn God's forgiveness; we can only accept it in perfect trust and faith.

(ii) Now that is to say that works have nothing to do with earning salvation. But that is precisely where it is neither right nor possible to leave the teaching of Paul—

and yet that is where it is so often left. Paul goes on to say that we are recreated by God for good works. Here is the Pauline paradox. All the good works in the world cannot put us right with God; but once we have been put right with God there is something radically wrong with the Christianity which does not issue in good works. There is nothing mysterious about this. This is simply an inevitable law of love. When anyone loves us, especially if that person is fine and lovely and splendid, we know that we cannot deserve that love. To deserve a love like that is quite impossible. It is a gift beyond all deserving. But at the same time we know with utter conviction that we must spend all life in *trying* to be worthy of that love. That is our relationship to God. Nothing that we can ever do can win or earn the favour and the love of God. That is God's free gift of grace to us which we can only humbly and trustfully and gratefully accept; but that does not mean to say that we do not need to do anything about it. It means that from that time forward all life is one long effort to show our gratitude and to try to deserve that love. Good works can never earn salvation; but there is something radically wrong if salvation does not produce good works. It is not our good works which put God in our debt; it is God's love which lays on us the obligation to show that we are trying throughout all life to be worthy of it.

We know what God wants us to do; God has prepared long beforehand the kind of life He wants us to live, and has told us about it in His book and through His Son. We cannot earn God's love; but we can and must show how grateful we are for it, by seeking with our whole hearts to live the kind of life which will bring joy to the heart of God.

B.C. AND A.D.

EPHESIANS 2: 11-22

So then remember, that once, as far as human descent goes, you were Gentiles; you were called the uncircumcision by those who laid claim to that circumcision which is a physical thing, and a thing produced by men's hands. Remember that at that time you had no hope of a Messiah; you were aliens from the society of Israel, and strangers from the covenants on which the promises were based; you had no hope; you were in the world without God. But, as things now are, because of what Christ Jesus has done, you who were once far off have been brought near, at the price of the blood of Christ. For it is He who is our peace; it is He who made both Jew and Gentile into one, and who broke down the middle wall of the barrier between, and destroyed the enmity by coming in the flesh, and wiped out the law of commandments with all its decrees. This He did that in Himself He might make the two into one new man, by making peace between them, and that He might reconcile both to God in one body through the Cross, after He had slain the enmity between them by what He did. So He came and preached peace to you who were afar off, and peace to them who were near, because, through Him, we both have the right of entry into the presence of the Father, for we come in the one Spirit. So then you are no longer strangers and foreigners resident in a land that is not their own, but you are fellow citizens with God's consecrated people and members of the family of God. It is on the foundation of the prophets and the apostles that you have been built up; and the corner stone is Christ Himself. All the building that is going on is being fitted together in Him, and it will go on growing until it becomes a holy temple in the Lord, a temple into which you too are built as part, that you may become the dwelling place of God, through the work of the Spirit.

BEFORE CHRIST CAME

Ephesians 2: 11, 12

So then remember, that once, as far as human descent goes, you were Gentiles; you were called the uncircumcision by those who laid claim to that circumcision

> which is a physical thing, and a thing produced by
> men's hands. Remember that at that time you had
> no hope of a Messiah; you were aliens from the society
> of Israel, and strangers from the covenants on which
> the promises were based; you had no hope; you were
> in the world without God.

IN this passage Paul speaks of the condition of the Gentiles
before Christ came. Paul was the apostle to the Gentiles,
but, at the same time, Paul never forgot the special and the
unique place of the Jews in the design and the revelation
of God. Here he is drawing the contrast between the life
of the Gentile and of the Jew.

(i) The Gentiles were called the uncircumcision by those
who laid claim to that circumcision which is a physical
and man-made thing. Here was the first of the great
divisions. The Jew had an immense contempt for the
Gentile. The Gentiles, said the Jews, were created by God
to be fuel for the fires of Hell. God, they said, loves only
Israel of all the nations that He had made. The best of
the serpents crush, they said, the best of the Gentiles
kill. It was not even lawful to render help to a Gentile
mother in her hour of sorest need, for that would simply
be to bring another Gentile into the world. Until Christ
came the Gentiles were an object of contempt to the Jews.
The barrier between them was absolute. If a Jewish boy
married a Gentile girl, or if a Jewish girl married a Gentile
boy, the funeral of that Jewish boy or girl was carried out.
Such contact with a Gentile was the equivalent of death.
Even to go into a Gentile house rendered a Jew unclean.
Before Christ the barriers were up; after Christ the barriers
were down. Before Christ there was no hope of unity;
in Christ the new unity had come.

(ii) The Gentiles had no hope of a Messiah; the Authorized Version has it that they were *without Christ*. That
is a perfectly possible translation; it might well be correct;
but the word *Christos* is not primarily a proper name at all,
although it has become one. It is an adjective meaning
the anointed one. It was kings who on their coronation

125

were, and still are, anointed; and thus the word *Christos*, which is the Greek literal translation of the Hebrew word *Messiah*, came to mean the Anointed One of God, the expected, the longed for, the prayed for King whom God would send into the world to vindicate His own and to bring in the golden age. Even in their sorest and their bitterest days the Jews never doubted that that Messiah would come. But the Gentiles had no such hope. They never knew of and never expected a Messiah. Now see the result of that difference. For the Jew history was always going somewhere; for the Jew, no matter what the present was like, the future was glorious; for the Jew all life was an appeal from an impossible present to a radiant future; that is to say, the Jewish view of history is essentially, inherently, innately optimistic. On the other hand for the Gentile history was going nowhere. The Stoics had worked out their theory of history, and to them history was cyclic. They believed that history went on for three thousand years; that then there came a cataclysm and a conflagration in which the whole universe was consumed in flames; and that then the whole process began all over again, and the same events and the same people exactly repeated themselves. There is all the difference in the world there. To the Gentile history was a progress to nowhere; to the Jew history was a march to God. To the Gentile life was literally not worth living; to the Jew life was the way to greater life. To the Gentile history was a circular treadmill; to the Jew history was the road to God. With the coming of Christ the Gentile entered into that new view of history in which a man is always on the way to God.

HOPELESS AND HELPLESS

Ephesians 2: 11, 12

(iii) STILL further, the Gentiles were aliens from the society of Israel. What does that mean? The name for the people of Israel was *ho hagios laos*, the *holy* people. Now we have seen that the basic meaning of this word *hagios* is *different*, separate from, other than. In what sense were the people of Israel different from other peoples? They were different in the sense that in the realest sense their only king was God. Other nations might be governed by democracy or aristocracy; Israel was a theocracy. Their governor was God. After his triumphs, the people came to Gideon and offered him the throne of Israel; for all that he had done, they would gladly make him king. Gideon's answer was: " I will not rule over you, neither shall my son rule over you; the Lord shall rule over you " (*Judges* 8: 23). When the Psalmist sang: " I will extol Thee, my God, O King " (*Psalm* 145: 1) he meant it perfectly literally. The Gentiles might be ruled over by kings and tyrants and rulers and unpredictable senates and councils; the king of Israel was God. To be an Israelite was to be a member of the society of God; it was to have a citizenship which was divine. Clearly life was going to be completely different for any nation which had a consciousness of destiny like that. It is told that when Pericles, the greatest of the Athenians, was walking forward to address the Athenian assembly, he used to say to himself : " Pericles, remember that you are an Athenian and that you talk to Athenians." But for the Jew it was possible to say: " Remember that you are a citizen of God, and that you speak to the people of God." There is no consciousness of greatness in all the world like that.

(iv) The Gentiles were strangers from the covenants on which the promises were based. What does that mean? Israel was supremely *the covenant people*. What does that mean? The Jewish idea of a covenant was this. They believed that God had approached their nation with a special offer. " I will take you to me for a people, and I will be to you a God " (*Exodus* 6: 7). This relationship involved not only privilege, it also involved obligation.

This covenant relationship involved the keeping of the law. The relationship depended on the people keeping and observing and obeying the law which God gave to them. *Exodus* 24: 1-8 gives us a dramatic picture of how the Jewish people accepted the covenant and its conditions— " All the words which the Lord hath said we will do " (*Exodus* 24: 3, 7). If God's design had ever to be worked out, it must be worked out through a nation. God's choice of Israel was not favouritism, for it was not choice for special honour; it was choice for special responsibility. But it gave to the Jews the peculiar and the unique consciousness of being the people of God. Simply to be a Jew was to have the consciousness of dignity. Paul could not forget, because it was a fact of history, that the Jews were uniquely the people of God, the instrument in God's hand.

(v) The Gentiles were without hope and without God in the world. People often speak of the Greeks as being the sunniest people in history; but there was such a thing as the Greek melancholy. At the back of things there was a kind of essential despair. Even as far back as Homer that is so. In the *Iliad* (6: 146-149) Glaucus and Diomede meet in single combat. Before they close in fight, Diomede wishes to know the lineage of Glaucus, and Glaucus replies: " Why enquirest thou of my generation? Even as are the generations of leaves such are those likewise of men; the leaves that be the wind scattereth upon the earth, and the forest buddeth and putteth forth more again, when the season of spring is at hand; so of the generations of men one putteth forth and another ceaseth." The Greek could say:

" We blossom and flourish as leaves on the tree,
    And wither and perish "—

But he could not triumphantly add:

" But nought changeth Thee."

Theognis could write:

> " I rejoice and disport me in my youth; long enough
> beneath the earth shall I lie, bereft of life, voiceless
> as a stone, and shall leave the sunlight which I
> loved; good man though I am, then shall I see
> nothing more."

> " Rejoice, O my soul, in thy youth; soon shall other
> men be in life, and I shall be black earth in death."

> " No mortal is happy of all on whom the sun looks
> down."

In the *Homeric Hymns* the assembly of Olympus is charmed
by the Muses who sing " of the deathless gifts of the gods
and the sorrows of men, even all that they endure by the
will of the immortals, living heedless and helpless, nor
can they find a cure for death, nor a defence against old
age." In Sophocles we find some of the loveliest and
the saddest lines in all history.

> " Youth's beauty fades, and manhood's glory fades.
> Faith dies and unfaith blossoms as a flower;
> Nor ever wilt thou find upon the open streets of men,
> Or secret places of the heart's own love,
> One wind blows true for ever."

It was true that the Gentile was without hope because he
was without God. Israel had always had the shining, radiant
hope in God, which burned clearly and inextinguishably
even in her darkest and most terrible days; but in his
heart the Gentile knew despair, before Christ came to give
him hope for hopelessness.

THE END OF BARRIERS

Ephesians 2: 13-18

> But as things now are, because of what Christ Jesus
> has done, you who were once far off have been brought
> near, at the price of the blood of Christ. For it is He
> who is our peace; it is He who made both Jew and
> Gentile into one, and who broke down the middle wall
> of the barrier between, and destroyed the enmity

by coming in the flesh, and wiped out the law of commandments with all its decrees. This He did that in Himself He might make the two into one new man, by making peace between them, and that He might reconcile both to God in one body through the Cross, after He had slain the enmity by what He did. So He came and preached peace to you who were afar off, and peace to them who were near, because, through Him, we both have the right of entry into the presence of the Father, for we come in the one Spirit.

WE have already seen how the Jews hated and despised the Gentile. Now Paul uses two pictures which would be specially vivid to a Jew to show how that hatred is killed and a new unity has come.

He says that those who were afar off had been brought near. Isaiah had heard God say: " Peace, peace to him that is afar off, and to him that is near " (*Isaiah* 57: 19). When the Rabbis spoke about accepting a convert into Judaism, they said that the proselyte to the faith had been *brought near*. For instance, the Jewish Rabbinic writers tell how a Gentile woman came to Rabbi Eliezer. She confessed that she was a sinner; she asked to be admitted to the Jewish faith. " Rabbi," she said, " bring me near." But the Rabbi refused; the door was shut in her face. But now the door was open; those who had been far from God were brought near, and the door was shut to no one.

But Paul uses an even more vivid picture. He says that the middle wall of the barrier between has been torn down. This is a picture from the Temple. The Temple consisted of a series of courts, each one a little higher than the one that went before, with the Temple itself in the inmost of the courts. First there was the Court of the Gentiles; then the Court of the Women; then the Court of the Israelites; then the Court of the Priests; and then the Holy Place itself. Only into the first of them could a Gentile come. Between it and the Court of the Women there was a wall, or rather a kind of screen of marble, beautifully wrought, and let into it at intervals there were tablets which announced that if a Gentile proceeded any farther he was liable to instant death. Josephus, in his description of the Temple, says: " When you go through these first cloisters unto the second court of the Temple, there was a partition made of stone all round, whose height was three cubits. Its construction was very elegant; upon it stood pillars at equal distances from one another, declaring the law of purity, some in Greek and some in Roman letters that no foreigner should go within the sanctuary " (*The Wars of the Jews*, 5, 5, 2). In another description he says of the second court of the Temple: " This was encompassed by a stone wall for a partition, with an inscription which forbade any foreigner to go in under pain of death " (*The Antiquities of the Jews*, 15, 11, 5). In 1871 one of these prohibiting tablets was actually discovered, and the inscription on it reads: " Let no one of any other nation come within the fence and barrier around the Holy Place. Whosoever will be taken doing so will himself be responsible for the fact that his death will ensue." Paul well knew that barrier, for his arrest at Jerusalem, the arrest which led to his final imprisonment and his death, was due to the fact that he himself had been wrongly accused of bringing Trophimus, an Ephesian Gentile, into the Temple beyond the barrier (*Acts* 21: 28, 29). So then the intervening wall with its unpassable barrier shut the Gentile out from the presence of God.

THE EXCLUSIVENESS OF CHRISTLESS HUMAN NATURE

Ephesians 2: 13-18 (*continued*)

IT is not to be thought that the Jews were the only people who put up the barriers and who shut people out. The ancient world was full of barriers. There was a time, more than four hundred years before this, when Greece was threatened with invasion by the Persians. At that time it was the golden age of the city state. Greece was made up of famous cities—Athens, Thebes, Corinth and the rest—and Greece very nearly encountered and even courted disaster because the cities refused to co-operate and come together to meet the common threat. " The danger lay," T. R. Glover wrote, " in every generation in the same fact of single cities, furious for independence at all costs." Cicero could write much later than that: " As the Greeks say, all men are divided into two classes—Greeks and barbarians." The Greek called any man a barbarian if he could not speak Greek, and they despised the barbarians and put up the barriers against them. When Aristotle is discussing bestiality, he says: " It is found most frequently among barbarians," and by barbarians he simply meant non-Greeks. He talks of " the remote tribes of barbarians belonging to the bestial class." The most vital form of Greek religion was the Mystery Religions, and from many of them the barbarian, the non-Greek, was excluded. Livy writes: " The Greeks wage a truceless war against people of other races, against barbarians." Plato said that the barbarians, the non-Greeks, are " our enemies by nature."

There is a Dutch proverb which says: " Unknown makes unloved," and in the ancient world the man of the other race was a potential and often an actual enemy. This problem of the barriers is by no means a problem that is confined to the ancient world. Rita Snowden quotes two very relevant sayings. Father Taylor of Boston used to say: " There is just enough room in the world for all the people in it, but there is no room for the fences which separate them." Sir Philip Gibbs in his book *The Cross of Peace* wrote of the modern situation: " The problem of fences has grown to be one of the most acute that the world must face. To-day there are all sorts of zig-zag and criss-crossing separating fences running through the races and people of the world. Modern progress has made the world a neighbourhood: God has given us the task of making it a brotherhood. In these days of dividing walls of race and class and creed we must shake the earth anew with the message of the all-inclusive Christ, in whom there is neither bond nor free, Jew nor Greek, Scythian nor barbarian, but all are one."

The ancient world had its fences and its barriers. The Jew hated all men, and regarded all men as hated by God except his own nation. The Greek ranked the barbarian with the beasts, and regarded a truceless war against him as written into the very nature of things. To-day there are still the iron curtains and the tariff barriers and the divisions between nation and nation, and class and class, colour and colour and Church and Church. In any Christless society there can be nothing but barriers and nothing but middle walls of partition.

THE UNITY IN CHRIST

Ephesians 2: 13-18 (*continued*)

So Paul goes on to say that in Christ these barriers are down. And how did Christ destroy them?

(i) Paul says of Jesus, " He is our peace." What did he mean by that? Let us use a human analogy. Suppose two people have a quarrel and a difference. Suppose they go to law about it, and suppose the experts in the law draw up a document, which states the rights of the case, and suppose they ask the two conflicting parties to come together on the basis of that document. In that case all the chances are that the quarrel will still go on and the breach will remain unhealed, for peace is seldom made on the basis of a legal document. But suppose that someone whom both of these conflicting parties love comes to them and talks to them and brings their hands and hearts together, then there is every chance that peace will be made. When two parties are at variance, the surest way to bring them together is through someone whom they both love.

That is what Christ does. *He* is our peace. It is in a common
love of Him that people come to love each other. And that
peace is won at the price of His blood, for the great awakener
of love is the Cross. It is on the Cross that He draws all
men unto Him (*John* 12: 32). The sight of that Cross
awakens in the hearts of men of all nations love for Christ,
and only when they all love Christ will they love each other.
It is not in treaties and discussions and leagues and societies
to beget peace. There can only be peace in Jesus Christ.

(ii) Paul says of Jesus that He wiped out the law of the
commandments with all its decrees. What does that mean?
The Jews believed that only by keeping the Jewish law
was a man good, and only by so doing could he attain to the
friendship and the fellowship of God. Now that law had
been worked out into thousands and thousands of rules
and regulations and commandments and decrees. Hands
had to be washed in a certain way; dishes had to be
cleaned in a certain way; there was page after page about
what could be done and what could not be done on the
Sabbath day; this and that and the next sacrifice had to be
offered in connection with this and that and the next
occasion in life. Clearly you could never make a universal
religion out of that. The only people who really and fully
kept the Jewish law were the Pharisees and there were
only six thousand of them. A religion which is based on
all kinds of rules and regulations, about sacred rituals and
customs and practices and sacrifices and days can never
be a universal religion. But, as Paul said, " Christ is the
end of the law " (*Romans* 10: 4); as he says here: " Jesus
wiped out the law of the commandments with all their
decrees." Jesus ended legalism as a principle of religion.

And what did He put in its place? He put love to God
and love to men. Jesus came to tell men that they cannot
earn God's approbation by a keeping of the ceremonial
law; that they must accept the love and forgiveness and
fellowship which God in mercy freely offers them. A
religion which is based on love can at once be a universal

religion. Rita Snowden tells a story of the war. In France
some soldiers with their sergeant brought the body of a
dead comrade to a French cemetery to have their friend
buried there. The priest told them gently that it was a
Roman Catholic cemetery, and he was bound to ask if
their comrade had been a baptized adherent of the Roman
Catholic Church. They said that they did not know. The
priest said that he was very sorry, but, if that was the case,
he could not permit burial in his churchyard. So the soldiers
took their comrade sadly and buried him just outside the
fence of the churchyard. The next day they came back to
see that the grave was all right, and to their astonishment
they could not find it. They knew that it was only six
feet from the fence of the burying ground, but search as they
might they could find no trace of the freshly dug soil.
As they were about to leave in perplexed bewilderment
the priest came up. He told them that his heart had been
troubled because of his refusal to allow their dead comrade
to be buried in the churchyard; so he told them that early
in the morning he had risen from his bed, and with his
own hands *he had moved the fence* to include the body of
the soldier who had died for France. That is what love
can do. The rules and the regulations put up the fence;
but love moved it. Jesus removed the fences between
man and man because He abolished all religion that is
founded on rules and regulations, and brought to men a
religion whose foundation is love.

THE GIFTS OF THE UNITY OF CHRIST

Ephesians 2: 13-18 (continued)

PAUL now goes on to tell of the priceless gifts which Christ
has brought to men, the gifts which come with the new
unity in Christ.

(i) He made both Jew and Gentile into one new man.
In Greek there are two words for new. There is *neos* which

is new simply in point of time; a thing which is *neos* is simply a thing which has come into existence recently; but there may well have been hundreds and thousands of exactly the same thing in existence before. A pencil which has been produced in the factory this week is new, in the sense of *neos*, but there already exist millions of pencils which are exactly like it. There is *kainos* which means not so much new in point of time, as new in point of *quality*. A thing which is *kainos* is new in the sense that it brings into the world a new kind of thing, a new quality of thing, which did not exist before. Now the word that Paul uses is *kainos*; he says that Jesus brings together Jew and Gentile and from them both produces one new kind of person. This is very interesting and very significant; it is not that Jesus makes all the Jews into Gentiles, or all the Gentiles into Jews; He produces a new kind of person out of both, although they remain Gentiles and Jews. Chrysostom, the famous preacher of the early Church, says that it is as if one should melt down a statue of silver and a statue of lead, and the two should come out gold. The unity which Jesus achieves is not achieved by blotting out all the racial and national characteristics; it is achieved by making all men of all nations into Christians. It may well be that we have something to learn here. The tendency has always been that when we send missionaries abroad we tend to produce people who wear English clothes and speak the English language and have an English education. There are indeed some missionary Churches who would have all their congregations worship with the one liturgy which is used in the Churches at home. But it is not Jesus' purpose that we should turn all men into one nation, but that there should be Christian Indians and Christian Africans, whose unity lies in their Christianity. The oneness in Christ is in Christ, and not in any external change.

(ii) He reconciled both to God. The word that Paul uses (*apokatallassein*) is the word which is used of bringing together friends who have been estranged. The work of Jesus is to show all men that God is their friend, and because God is their friend, that they must be friends with each other. Reconciliation with God involves and necessitates reconciliation with man.

(iii) Through Jesus both Jew and Gentile have the right of access to God. The word which Paul uses for *access* is the word *prosagōgē* and it is a word of many pictures. It is the word used of bringing a sacrifice to God; it is the word used of bringing men into the presence of God that they may be consecrated to His service; it is the word used for introducing a speaker or an ambassador into a national assembly; and above all it is the word used for introducing a person into the presence of a king. There was in fact at the Persian royal court an official called the *prosagōgeus* whose function it was to introduce people who desired an audience with the king. It is a priceless boon to have the right to go to some lovely and wise and saintly person at any time; to have the right to break in upon him, to disturb him, to take our troubles, our problems, our loneliness, our sorrow to him. That is exactly the right that Jesus gives us in regard to God. Because of Jesus the door is always open to the presence of God for Jew and for Gentile alike.

The unity in Christ produces Christians whose Christianity transcends all their local and racial difference; it produces men who are friends with each other because they are friends with God; it produces men who are one, because they meet in the presence of God to whom they all have access.

THE FAMILY AND THE DWELLING-PLACE OF GOD

Ephesians 2: 19-22

So then you are no longer strangers and foreigners resident in a land that is not their own, but you are

> fellow citizens with God's consecrated people and
> members of the family of God. It is on the foundation
> of the prophets and apostles that you have been built
> up; and the corner stone is Christ Himself. All the
> building that is going on is being fitted together in
> Him, and it will go on growing until it becomes a
> holy temple in the Lord, a temple into which you too
> are built as part, that you may become the dwelling-
> place of God, through the work of the Spirit.

IN this last section of this chapter Paul uses two illuminating
pictures. He says that the Gentiles are no longer strangers
and foreigners, but full citizens amidst God's people and
full members of the family of God.

Paul uses the word *xenos* for foreigner. In every Greek
city there were *xenoi*, and their life was not easy. A man
who was a stranger in a strange city writes home: " It is
better for you to be in your own homes, whatever they
may be like, than to be in a strange land." The foreigner
was always regarded with suspicion and dislike. Paul
uses the word *paroikos* for sojourner. The *paroikos* was
one step further on. He was a resident alien; he was a
man who had come to stay in a place but who had never
become a naturalized citizen; he paid a tax for the privilege
of existing in a land which was not his own. He might
stay there and he might work there, but he was a stranger
and an outsider whose home was somewhere else. Both
the *xenos* and the *paroikos* were where they were on sufferance; they were always on the fringe.

So Paul says to the Gentiles: " You are no longer in the
Church and among God's people on sufferance. You are
real citizens of the society of God. You are full members
of the family of God." We may put this very simply;
it is through Jesus that we are at home with God. A. B.
Davidson tells how he was in lodgings in a strange city.
He was lonely. He used to walk the streets at evening time;
and sometimes through an uncurtained window he would see
a family sitting round the table or the fire in happy fellowship; and then the curtain would be drawn and he would

138

feel shut out, and lonely in the dark. That is what cannot happen in the family of God. And that is what should never happen in a Church. Through Jesus there is a seat and a place for every one of us, and for all men, in the family of God. Men may put up their barriers; Churches may keep their Communion tables for their own members; God never does; it is the tragedy of the Church that it is so often more exclusive than God.

The second picture that Paul uses is the picture of a building. He thinks of every Church as the part of a great building and of every Christian as a stone built into the Church. And of the whole Church the corner stone is Christ; if you take the corner stone away the whole arch will collapse in rubble; it is the corner stone which holds everything together.

Paul thinks of this building going on and on, and each part of the building is fitted into Christ. Think of what a great Cathedral is often like. Down among the foundations there may be a Saxon crypt; on some of the doorways or the windows there may be a Norman arch; one part of it may be Early English and another Decorated and another Gothic; some of it may have been added in our own lifetime and in our own day. There are all kinds of architecture; all kinds of men built it; but the building is a unity because through it all and in it all it has been used for the worship of God and for meeting with Jesus Christ.

That is what the Church should be like. Its unity comes not from organization, or ritual, or liturgy, or worship. Its unity comes from Christ. In the Latin phrase *ubi Christus, ibi ecclesia*, Where Christ is, there is the Church. The Church will only realize her unity when she realizes that she does not exist to propagate the point of view of any body of men, but to give a home and a dwelling-place where the Spirit of Christ can dwell, and where all men who love Christ can meet in that Spirit.

PRISON AND PRIVILEGES

EPHESIANS 3: 1-13

To understand the connection of thought in this passage
it has to be noted that verses 2-13 are one long parenthesis.
The *for this cause* of verse 14 takes up again and resumes
the *for this cause* of verse 1. Someone has spoken of Paul's
habit of " going off at a word." A single word or idea
can send Paul's thoughts off at a tangent. When Paul
speaks of himself as " the prisoner of Christ," it makes
him think of the discovery of the universal love of God,
and his part in the bringing of that love to the Gentiles.
In verses 2-13 his thoughts go off on that track; and then
in verse 14 he comes back to what he meant to say when
he began.

It is for this cause that I Paul, the prisoner of Jesus
Christ for the sake of you Gentiles—you must have heard
of the share that God gave me in dispensing His grace to
you, because God's secret was made known to me by direct
revelation, as I have just been writing to you, and you can
read again what I have just written, if you wish to know
what I understand of the meaning of that secret which
Christ brought, a secret which was not revealed to the sons
of men in other generations as it has now been revealed to
His consecrated apostles and prophets by the work of the
Spirit. The secret is that the Gentiles are fellow-heirs,
fellow-members of the same body, fellow-sharers in the
promise in Jesus Christ, through the good news of which
I was made a servant through the free gift of the grace
of God, which was given to me according to the working
of His power. It is to me, who am less than the least of all
God's consecrated people, that this privilege has been
given—the privilege of preaching to the Gentiles the wealth
of Christ, the full story of which no man can ever tell;
the privilege of enlightening all men as to what is the
meaning of that secret, which was hidden from all eternity,
in the God who created all things. It was kept secret up
till now in order that now the many-coloured wisdom of
God should be made known through the Church to the
rulers and powers in the heavenly places; and all this
happened and will happen in accordance with the eternal

design which He purposed in Jesus Christ, through whom we have a free and confident right of approach to Him through faith in Him. I therefore pray that you will not lose heart because of my afflictions on your behalf, for these afflictions are your glory.

THE GREAT DISCOVERY

Ephesians 3: 1-7

> It is for this cause that I Paul, the prisoner of Jesus Christ for the sake of you Gentiles—you must have heard of the share that God gave me in dispensing His grace to you, because God's secret was made known to me by direct revelation, as I have just been writing to you, and you can read again what I have just written, if you wish to know what I understand of the meaning of that secret which Christ brought, a secret which was not revealed to the sons of men in other generations as it has now been revealed to His consecrated apostles and prophets by the work of the Spirit. The secret is that the Gentiles are fellow-heirs, fellow-members of the same body, fellow-sharers in the promise in Jesus Christ, through the good news of which I was made a servant through the free gift of the grace of God, which was given to me according to the working of His power.

WHEN Paul wrote this letter he was in prison in Rome awaiting trial before Nero. He was waiting for the Jewish prosecutors to come with their bleak faces and their envenomed hatred and their malicious charges. It is true that in prison Paul had certain privileges, for he was allowed to stay in the house which he himself had rented, and his friends were allowed access to him; but, even then, night and day he was a prisoner; night and day he was chained by a length of chain to the wrist of the Roman soldier who was his guard, and whose duty it was to see that Paul would never escape. In these circumstances Paul calls himself " the prisoner of Christ." Here is another vivid instance of the fact that the Christian has always a double life and a double address. Any ordinary person

looking at Paul in prison, would have said that Paul was
the prisoner of the Roman government; and so in one
sense he was; but Paul never thought of himself as the
prisoner of Rome; he always thought of himself as the
prisoner of Christ. He did not think of himself as arrested
by the Roman authorities; he thought of himself as suffering for the sake of Christ. A point of view makes all the
difference in the world. There is a famous story of the
days when Sir Christopher Wren was building St. Paul's
Cathedral. On one occasion Sir Christopher Wren was
making a tour of the work in progress. He came upon a
man at work and asked him: "What are you doing?"
The man said: "I am cutting this stone to a certain
size and shape." He came to a second man and asked
him what he was doing. The man said: "I am earning
so much money at my work." He came to a third man at
work and asked him what he was doing. The man paused
for a moment in his work, and straightened himself and
answered: "I am helping Sir Christopher Wren to build
St. Paul's Cathedral." There was all the difference in the
world in the point of view of these three men. If a man is
in prison for some great cause he may either grumblingly
regard himself as a poor and wretched and ill-used creature,
or he may radiantly regard himself as the standard-bearer
and protagonist of some great cause. The one man will
regard his prison as a penance; the other man will regard
it as a privilege. When we are undergoing hardship,
unpopularity, material loss for the sake of Christian
principles we can either regard ourselves as the victims
of men, or as the champions of Christ. Our point of view
will make all the difference. Paul is our example; he
regarded himself, not as the prisoner of Nero, but as the
prisoner of Christ.

In this section Paul recurs to the thought which is at
the very heart of this letter. Into his life there had come
the revelation of the great secret of God. That secret
was that the love and the mercy and the grace of God were

meant, not for the Jews alone, but for all mankind. When
Paul had met Christ on the Damascus road there had come
to him a sudden flash of revelation. It was to the Gentiles
that God had sent him " to open their eyes and to turn
them from darkness to light, and from the power of Satan
unto God, that they may receive forgiveness of sins, and
inheritance among them which are sanctified by faith that is
in God." (*Acts* 26: 18). This was a completely new discovery.
The basic sin of the ancient world was contempt. The Jews
despised the Gentiles who were useless and worthless—
so they thought—in the sight of God. At the worst the
Gentiles existed only to be annihilated. " The nation
and kingdom that will not serve thee shall perish; yea
those nations shall be utterly wasted " (*Isaiah* 60: 12).
At the best the Gentiles existed to be the slaves of Israel.
" The labour of Egypt and the merchandise of Ethiopia
and of the Sabeans, men of stature, shall come over unto
thee and they shall be thine; they shall come after thee;
in chains they shall come over and they shall fall down
unto thee " (*Isaiah* 45: 14). To minds which could think
like that it was incredible that the grace and the glory
of God were for the Gentiles. The Greek despised the
barbarians of other nations—and to the Greek all other
nations were barbarians. As Celsus said when he was
attacking the Christians, " the barbarians may have
some gift for discovering truth, but it takes a Greek to
understand." This racial and national contempt did not
end with the ancient world. In the sixteenth century
Complaynt of Scotland, it is written: " Euere nation
reputis vthers nations to be barbarianes, quhen there twa
natours and complexions ar contrar till vtheris." To this
day the Chinese refer contemptuously to all foreigners as
barbarians. In the *Mercantile Marine Magazine* of 1858
there is a recommendation to the effect that the term
barbarian should not be applied to British subjects in
Chinese official documents. (These two illustrations are
taken from *The Stranger at the Gate*, by T. J. Haarhoff.)

But in the ancient world the barriers were complete. No one had ever dreamed that God's grace and privileges and love were for all people. It was Paul who made that discovery. That is why Paul is so tremendously important— for, had there been no Paul it is quite conceivable that there would have been no world-wide Christianity, and that we would not be Christians to-day.

THE SELF-CONSCIOUSNESS OF PAUL

Ephesians 3: 1-7 (*continued*)

WHEN Paul thought of this secret of God which had been revealed to him, he thought of himself in certain ways.

(i) He regarded himself as the recipient of a new revelation. We must note that Paul never thought of himself as having *discovered* the universal love of God; he thought of God having *revealed* it to him. There is a sense in which truth and beauty are always given by God. Truth and beauty are not so much man's discovery as God's gift. It is told that once Sir Arthur Sullivan was at a performance of his own opera *H.M.S. Pinafore*. When that lovely duet "*Ah! Leave me not to pine alone*" had been sung, Sullivan turned to the friend who was sitting beside him and said, " Did I really write that? " One of the great examples of poetical music of words in literature is Coleridge's *Kubla Khan*. Coleridge fell asleep reading a book in which there were the words: " Here Kubla Khan commanded a place to be built and a stately garden thereunto." He dreamed the poem and when he awoke he had nothing to do but to write it down. When a scientist makes a great discovery, over and over again what happens is that he thinks and thinks, and experiments and experiments, and then comes to a dead end. Human thought and human ingenuity will go no further. And then quite suddenly the solution to his problem flashes upon him. It is not thought out; it is given to him—by God. Paul would never have claimed to be the first man to discover the universality of the love

144

of God; he would have said that God told him the secret
which had not been hitherto revealed to any man.

(ii) He regarded himself as the transmitter of grace.
When Paul met the leaders of the Church to talk over
with them his mission to the Gentiles, he talks about the
gospel of the uncircumcision being committed unto him;
and he talks of " the grace which was given unto me "
(*Galatians* 2: 7, 9). When he writes to the Romans, he
speaks of " the grace that is given to me of God " (*Romans*
15: 15). Paul saw his task in this life as the task of being
a channel of God's grace to men. He was the pipe-line
through which the grace of God was to come to men.
It is one of the great facts of the Christian life that we
were given the precious things of Christianity in order
that we might share them with others. It is one of the
great warnings of the Christian life that if we keep them to
ourselves we lose them. We keep them only by passing
them on.

(iii) He regarded himself as having the dignity of service.
He says that he was made a servant by the free gift of the
grace of God. To Paul the biggest glory that he had was
the task laid on him by God. He did not think of his service
as a wearisome duty; he thought of it as a radiant privilege.
It is so often so very difficult to persuade people to serve
the Church. To teach for God, to sing for God, to administer
the affairs of a congregation for God, to speak for God,
to visit those in poverty and distress for God, to give of
our time and our strength and our substance for God, is
not a duty which ought to be coerced out of us; it is a
privilege which we should regard as the gift of the grace
of God.

(iv) Paul regarded himself as the sufferer for Christ.
He did not expect the way of service to be an easy way;
he did not expect the way of loyalty to be a trouble-free
way. Unamuno, the great Spanish mystic, used to say,
" May God deny you peace, and give you glory." F. R.
Maltby used to say that Jesus promised His disciples

three things—that " they would be absurdly happy, completely fearless, and in constant trouble." When the knights of the days of chivalry came to the court of King Arthur and to the society of the Round Table, they came asking for dangers to face and dragons to conquer. To suffer for Christ is not a penalty; it is our glory, for it is to share in the sufferings of Christ Himself and it is an opportunity to demonstrate the reality of our loyalty to Him.

THE PRIVILEGE WHICH MAKES A MAN HUMBLE

Ephesians 3: 8-13

> It is to me, who am less than the least of all God's consecrated people, that this privilege has been given —the privilege of preaching to the Gentiles the wealth of Christ, the full story of which no man can ever tell; the privilege of enlightening all men as to what is the meaning of that secret, which was hidden from all eternity, in the God who created all things. It was kept secret up till now in order that now the many-coloured wisdom of God should be made known through the Church to the rulers and powers in the heavenly places; and all this happened and will happen in accordance with the eternal design which He purposed in Jesus Christ, through whom we have a free and confident approach to Him through faith in Him. I therefore pray that you will not lose heart because of my afflictions on your behalf, for these afflictions are your glory.

PAUL saw himself as a man who had been given a double privilege. He had been given the privilege of discovering the secret that it was God's will that all men should be gathered into the secret of His grace and love. And he had been given the privilege of making this secret known to the Church, and of being the instrument whereby God's grace went out to the Gentiles. But that consciousness of privilege did not make Paul proud; it made him intensely humble. He was amazed that this great privilege had been

given to him who, as he saw it, was less than the least of
God's people. If ever we are privileged to preach or to
teach the message of the love of God, or to do anything
for Jesus Christ in His Church, we must always remember
that our greatness lies, not in ourselves, but in our task
and in our message. Toscanini was one of the greatest
orchestral conductors and interpreters of music in the
world. Once when he was talking to an orchestra when he
was preparing to play one of Beethoven's symphonies
with them he said: " Gentlemen, I am nothing; you
are nothing; Beethoven is everything." He knew well
that his duty was not to draw attention to himself or to
his orchestra; his duty was to obliterate himself and his
orchestra and to let Beethoven flow through. Leslie
Weatherhead somewhere tells of a talk he had with a public
schoolboy who had decided to enter the ministry of the
Church. He asked him when he had come to his decision,
and the lad said he had been moved to make it after a
certain service in the school chapel. Leslie Weatherhead
very naturally asked who the preacher had been, and the
lad answered that he had no idea who the preacher was;
he only knew that Jesus Christ had spoken to him that
morning. That was true preaching; for he who serves
Christ can never think of making others look at himself
and praise himself; he must make them look at Christ.
The tragic fact in Churches is that there are so many who
are more concerned with their own honour and prestige
than with the honour and the prestige of Jesus Christ;
and who are more concerned that they should be noticed
than that Christ should be seen.

THE PLAN AND THE WISDOM OF GOD

Ephesians 3: 8-13 (*continued*)

THERE are still other things in this passage which we
must note.

   (i) Paul here reminds us that the ingathering of all men

of all nations was part of the eternal purpose and design of God. That is something which we would do well to remember. Sometimes the history of Christianity can be presented in such a way that it sounds as if the gospel went out to the Gentiles only because the Jews would not receive it. But Paul here reminds us that the salvation of the Gentiles, our own salvation, is not an afterthought of God; it is not something which God accepted as a second best, because the Jews rejected His message and His invitation. The bringing of all men into His love was part of the eternal design of God.

(ii) Paul here uses a great word to describe the grace of God. He calls it *polupoikilos*, which means *many-coloured*. The idea in this word is that the grace of God will match with any situation which life may bring to us. There is nothing of light or of dark, of sunshine or of shadow, for which this grace of God is not triumphantly adequate.

(iii) Once again Paul returns to one of his favourite thoughts. In Jesus we have a free approach to God. It sometimes happens that some friend of ours knows some very distinguished person. We ourselves would never have any right to enter into that person's presence; but our friend takes us in, and in our friend's company we have the right of entry. That is what Jesus does for us with God. In His presence and in His company there is an open door to the presence of God which no man can ever shut.

(iv) Paul finishes with a prayer that his friends may not be discouraged by his imprisonment. It might be that they might think that the preaching of the gospel to the Gentiles might be greatly hindered because the champion of the Gentiles was in prison. It might be that they might be afraid lest a like fate should befall them. Paul reminds them that the afflictions through which he is going are for their glory and for their good. They need never fear that God's cause will be handicapped because Paul is in prison. God's cause is greater than any man.

PAUL'S EARNEST PRAYER

EPHESIANS 3: 14-21

IT is for this cause that I bow my knees in prayer before the Father, of whose fatherhood all heavenly and earthly fatherhood is a copy, that, according to the wealth of His glory, He may grant to you to be strengthened in the inner man, so that Christ through faith may take up His permanent residence in your hearts. I pray that you may have your root and your foundation in love, so that, with all God's consecrated people, you may have the strength fully to grasp the meaning of the breadth and length and depth and height of Christ's love, and to know the love of Christ which is beyond all knowledge, that you may be filled until you reach the fullness of God Himself.

To Him that is able to do exceeding abundantly, above all that we ask or think, according to the power which works in us, to Him be glory in the Church and in Christ Jesus to all generations for ever and ever. Amen.

THE GOD WHO IS FATHER

Ephesians 3: 14-17

It is for this cause that I bow my knees in prayer before the Father, of whose fatherhood all heavenly and earthly fatherhood is a copy, that, according to the wealth of His glory, He may grant to you to be strengthened in the inner man, so that Christ through faith may take up His permanent residence in your hearts.

IT is here that Paul begins again the sentence which he began in verse I and from which he was deflected and which he never finished. *It is for this cause* begins Paul. What is the cause of which he speaks, and the cause which makes him pray? Here we are back again at the basic idea of the whole letter. Paul has painted his great picture of the Church. This world is a disintegrated chaos; there is division and separation everywhere, between nation and nation, between man and man, within a man's inner life. It is God's design that all the warring and the discordant elements should be brought into one in Jesus Christ. Jesus is God's instrument whereby men are to be brought into one. But that cannot be done unless the Church carries the message of Christ and of the love of God to every man. The Church is to be the complement of Christ, the body through which the Spirit of Christ acts and operates. It is for that cause that Paul prays. If the Church is ever to be like that, the people within it must be a certain kind of people. That is why Paul is praying; he is praying that the people within the Church may be such that the whole Church will be in truth the body and the complement of Christ.

We must note the word which is used for Paul's attitude in prayer. " I bow my knees," he says, " in prayer to God." That means even more than that Paul kneels in prayer; it means that he prostrates himself in prayer before God. The ordinary Jewish attitude of prayer was standing, with the hands stretched out with the palms upwards; but Paul's prayer for the Church is so intense that he prostrates himself before God in an agony of entreaty.

Paul's prayer is to God the Father. It is interesting to note the different things which Paul says in this letter about God as Father, for from them we get a clearer idea of what was in Paul's mind when he spoke of the fatherhood of God.

(i) God is the Father of Jesus (1: 2, 3; 1: 17; 6: 23). It is not true to say that Jesus was the first person to call God Father. The Greeks called Zeus the father of gods and men; the Romans called their chief god Jupiter, which means *Deus pater*, God the Father. But there are two closely interrelated words which have a certain similarity, and yet a wide difference in their significance. There is the word *paternity*. Paternity means fatherhood in the purely physical sense of the term. Paternity can be used of a fatherhood in which the father never even saw the child. A child might be born—perhaps illegitimately— and then immediately adopted by someone else. The father might never even see the child, but the father would be responsible for the paternity of the child, because he was responsible for the child's physical creation. On the other hand there is the word *fatherhood*. The word fatherhood describes the most intimate relationship of love and of fellowship and of care. When men used the word *father* of God before Jesus came, they used it much more in the sense of paternity. They meant that the gods were responsible for the creation of men. They meant much more what we would mean by the First Cause or the Life Force. There was in the word none of the love and intimacy which Jesus put into it. The centre of the Christian conception of God is that God is like Jesus, that God is as kind, as loving, as merciful as Jesus was. To Paul God was not just God; that might mean anything or nothing; God was the Father of Jesus Christ. It was always in terms of Jesus that Paul thought of God.

(ii) God is the <u>Father to whom we have access</u> (2: 18; 3: 12). The whole essence of the Old Testament is that God was the person to whom access was forbidden. When Manoah, who was to be the father of Samson, realized who his visitor had been, he said: " We shall surely die because we have seen God " (*Judges* 13: 22). In the Jewish worship of the Temple the Holy of Holies was held to be the dwelling-place of God; and into it only the High Priest might enter, and he might enter only on one day of the year, the Day of Atonement. The way to God was barred. The very centre of the Christian belief is the approach-ability of God. H. L. Gee tells a war story. There was a little boy whose father was promoted to the exalted rank of Brigadier. When the little lad heard the news, he was silent for a moment, and then said, "Do you think he will mind if I still call him daddy?" The essence of the Christian faith is the unrestricted access we have to the presence of God.

(iii) God is the Father of glory, the glorious Father (3: 14). Here is the necessary other side of the matter. If we simply spoke about the accessibility of God, if we simply insisted that God was like Jesus in His love and gentleness and mercy, it would be easy to sentimentalize the love of God, and that is exactly what some people do. Consciously or unconsciously, their attitude is: "God is Father; I don't need to worry; everything will be all right." But the Christian faith rejoices in the wonder of the accessibility of God without ever forgetting the holiness and the glory of God. It is not to a soft and easy-going and sentimental father that we have access. It is to the God of glory Himself. God welcomes the sinner, but not the sinner who trades on God's love in order to remain a sinner. God is holy and those who seek His friendship must be holy too. Our right of access to God does not give us the right to be and to do what we like. It lays upon us the obligation of seeking to be worthy of such a privilege.

(iv) God is the Father of all (6: 4). No man, no Church, no nation has exclusive possession of God. That is precisely the mistake which the Jews made. The fatherhood of God extends to all men, and therefore all human contempt and all human pride and all religious exclusiveness are necessarily wrong. The very fact of the fatherhood of God means that we must love and respect one another.

(v) God is the Father to whom thanks must be given (6: 20). The fatherhood of God implies the debt of man. It is quite wrong to think of God as helping us only in the great and crucial moments of life. It is our shame that because God's gifts come to us so regularly and so unfailingly we tend to forget that they are gifts. The Christian is a man who never forgets his debt to God, who never forgets that he owes, not only the salvation of his soul, but also life and breath and all things to God.

(vi) God is the pattern of all true fatherhood. Paul says that God is the Father of whose fatherhood all fatherhood in heaven and upon earth is a copy. That lays a tremendous responsibility on all human fathers. G. K. Chesterton remembered his father only vaguely, but his memories were very precious. He tells us that in his childhood he possessed a toy theatre in which all the characters were cut-outs in cardboard. One of them was a man with a golden key. He never could remember what the man with the golden key stood for in the characters of the theatre, but in his own mind he always connected his father with that character. To him his father was a man with a golden key opening to him all kinds of wonderful and of thrilling things. We can never afford to forget that we teach our children to call God father, and the only conception of fatherhood that they can have is the conception which we give them. Human fatherhood should be moulded and modelled on the pattern of the fatherhood of God. It is the tremendous duty of the human father to be as good a father as God.

THE STRENGTHENING OF CHRIST

Ephesians 3: 14-17 (*continued*)

IT is Paul's prayer that his people may be strengthened *in the inner man*. What did Paul mean by that? *The inner man* was a phrase which the Greeks knew and used. By *the inner man* the Greeks understood three things. (*a*) There was a man's *reason*. It is Paul's prayer that Jesus Christ should strengthen the reason of his friends. He wanted them to be better able to discern between that

which was right and that which was wrong. He wanted
them to be less at the mercy of their passions and their
instincts and their desires. He wanted Christ to give them
the wisdom which would keep life pure and safe. (*b*) There
was the *conscience*. It was Paul's prayer that the conscience
of his people should ever become more and more sensitive.
It is possible to disregard conscience so long and often
that in the end conscience becomes dulled and insensitive.
It was the prayer of Paul that Jesus should keep our
consciences tender and on the alert. (*c*) There was the
will. It is the essential weakness of life that so often we
know what is right, and we mean to do it, but our will
is not strong enough to back our knowledge and to carry
out our intentions. As John Drinkwater wrote:

> " Grant us the will to fashion as we feel,
>   Grant us the strength to labour as we know,
>   Grant us the purpose, ribbed and edged with steel,
>   To strike the blow.
>
> Knowledge we ask not, knowledge Thou hast lent,
>   But, Lord, the will—there lies our deepest need,
>   Grant us the power to build, above the high intent,
>   The deed, the deed! "

The inner man is the reason, the conscience, the will.

And how does Paul pray that the inner man should be
strengthened? The strengthening of the inner man comes
when Christ takes up His permanent residence in the man.
The word that Paul uses for Christ *dwelling* in our hearts
is the Greek word *katoikein* which is the word used for
permanent, as opposed to temporary, residence. Henry
Lyte wrote as one of the verses of the hymn *Abide with me*:

> " Not a brief glance I beg, a passing word,
>   But as Thou dwell'st with Thy disciples, Lord,
>   Familiar, condescending, patient, free,
>   Come, not to sojourn, but abide with me."

The secret of strength is the presence of Christ within
our lives. And Christ will come into a man's life—but He
will never force His way in. He will only come when we

ask Him to come. Christ awaits our invitation to bring to us His strength.

THE INFINITE LOVE OF CHRIST

Ephesians 3: 18-21

IT is Paul's prayer that the Christian may be able to grasp the meaning of the breadth, depth, length and height of the love of Christ. It is as if Paul invited us to look at the universe—to the limitless sky above, to the limitless horizons on every side, to the depth of the earth and the seas beneath us, and said, " The love of Christ is as wide as that."

It is not likely that Paul had any more definite thought in his mind than the sheer vastness of the love of Christ. But many people have taken this picture and have read meanings, some of them very beautiful, into it. One ancient commentator sees the Cross as the symbol of this love. The upper arm of the Cross points up; the lower arm of the Cross points down; and the crossing arms of the Cross point out to the widest horizons beyond the range of the eye to see. Jerome said that the love of Christ reaches up, to include the holy angels; that it reaches down to include even the evil spirits and devils in hell; that in its length it covers the men who are striving on the upward way; and in its breadth it covers the men who are drifting and wandering away from Christ on evil paths. If we wish to work this out we might say that in the *breadth* of its sweep, the love of Christ includes every man of every kind in every age in every world; in the *length* to which it would go, the love of Christ was obedient unto death and accepted even the Cross; in its *depth* it descended to experience even death; in its *height*, He still loves us in heaven, where He still ever liveth to make intercession for us (*Hebrews* 7: 25). There is no man who is outside the love of Christ; there is no place which is outwith the reach of Christ; there is no experience which the love of Christ will refuse in order to gain one man. It is a love which passes knowledge, and which, if he accepts it, will fill a man with nothing less than the life of God Himself.

And then Paul comes back again to the thought which dominates this epistle and which is for ever recurring all through it. Where is that love to be experienced? How are we to grasp it and find it and enter into it? We find it and we experience it *with all God's consecrated people*. That is to say, we find it in the fellowship of the Church. John Wesley's saying was true, " God knows nothing of solitary religion." " No man," he said, " ever went to heaven alone." The Church may have its faults; the church members may be very far from being the people they ought to be; but in the fellowship of the Church we find the love of God.

So Paul ends with a doxology and an ascription of praise. God can do for us more than we can think or dream of, and he does it for us in the Church and in Christ.

So once again, before we leave this chapter, let us think of Paul's glorious picture of the Church. This world is not what it was meant to be; it is a world torn in sunder by opposing forces and by bitterness and hatred and strife. Nation is against nation, man is against man, class is against class. Within a man's own self the fight rages between the evil and the good. It is God's design that all men and all nations should become one in Christ. To make that day come true Christ needs the Church to go out and to tell men of His love and of His mercy. The Church is the complement of Christ, the Body of Christ, hands and feet and a voice to do Christ's work. And the Church cannot do that, until its members, joined together in fellowship, know and experience the limitless love of Christ. No man can teach another what he does not know, or give to another that which he does not possess. And before we can bring Christ's love to others we must find Christ's love within Christ's Church.

EPHESIANS 4

WITH this chapter the second part of the letter begins. In the first three chapters Paul has dealt with the great and eternal truths of the Christian faith, and with the function of the Church in the plan and the design of God. Now he begins to sketch what each member of the Church must be if the Church is to carry out her part in the plan and the purpose of God. Before we begin to read this chapter, let us again remind ourselves of the central thought of the whole letter. In this world there is nothing but discord, disharmony and disunity. Nation is divided against nation, and man against man; class is divided against class, and in man himself there goes on an inner and an unceasing battle between the higher and the lower part of his nature. It is God's design and God's purpose that all this disunity and disharmony should be resolved in Christ, that all men and all nations should become one in Christ, that in Christ the differences should be abolished and the separating walls torn down. It is God's aim that in Christ there should enter into the world what H. C. G. Moule called " a sacred oneness," and what, in modern language, we could call " a new togetherness." Jesus Christ supplies the one centre around whom and in whom all men can be gathered into one. But if ever that oneness is to be achieved and attained, the message of Christ, the fact of Christ, the love and the mercy and the seeking heart of God in Christ, must be taken out to the whole world. And it is the function of the Church to take that message and that love to men. The Church must be the body through which Christ acts and the voice through which He speaks. The Church must be Christ's instrument in bringing this divine unity into the world. But if the Church is to succeed in that great task, the people within the Church must be a certain kind of people. And now Paul turns to the character of the Christian which is necessary if the Church is to fulfil her great task of being

Christ's instrument of universal reconciliation between man and man, and man and God within the world.

WORTHY OF OUR CALLING

EPHESIANS 4: 1-10

So then, I, the prisoner in the Lord, urge you to behave yourselves in a way that is worthy of the calling with which you are called. I urge you to behave with all humility, and gentleness, and patience. I urge you to bear with one another in love. I urge you eagerly to preserve that unity which the Holy Spirit can bring by binding things together in peace. There is one body and one Spirit, just as you have been called with one hope of your calling. There is one Lord, one faith, one baptism, one God and Father of all, who is above all, and through all, and in all. To each one of you grace has been given, as it has been measured out to you by the free gift of Christ. Therefore scripture says, " He ascended into the height, and brought His captive band of prisoners, and gave gifts to men." (When it says that " He ascended," what else can it mean than that He also descended into the lower parts of the earth? He who descended is the same person as He who ascended above all the heavens, that He might fill all things with His presence.)

THE CHRISTIAN VIRTUES

Ephesians 4: 1-3

> So then, I, the prisoner in the Lord, urge you to behave yourselves in a way that is worthy of the calling with which you are called. I urge you to behave with all humility, and gentleness, and patience. I urge you to bear with one another in love. I urge you eagerly to preserve that unity which the Holy Spirit can bring by binding things together in peace.

WHEN a man enters into any society or into any fellowship, he takes upon himself the obligation to live a certain kind of life; and if he fails to live the kind of life which is necessary, he hinders the aims of his society, and he brings discredit on its name. So here Paul paints the picture of the kind of life that a man must live when he enters the fellowship of the Christian Church.

The first three verses of this passage shine with words which are like jewels. Here we have five of the great basic words of the Christian faith. Let us look at them one by one.

(i) First, and foremost, there is the word *humility*. The word for *humility* is *tapeinophrosunē*, and this word is actually a word which the Christian faith coined. It is true to say that in Greek there is no word for humility which has not some suggestion of meanness attaching to it. Later Basil was to describe humility as " the gem casket of all the virtues." But in the ancient world before Christianity humility was not counted as a virtue at all. The heathen virtue is *megalopsuchia* which means *great-heartedness*. The ancient world looked on humility as a cowering, cringing thing to be despised and not to be desired. The Greek had an adjective for *humble*, which is closely connected with this noun—the adjective *tapeinos*. A word is always known by the company it keeps and this word keeps ignoble company. It is used in company with the Greek adjectives which mean slavish (*andrapodōdēs*, *doulikos*, *douloprepēs*), ignoble (*agennēs*), of no repute (*adoxos*), cringing (*chamaizēlos*, which is the adjective which describes a plant which trails along the ground). Always in the days before Jesus, humility was looked on as a cowering, cringing, servile, ignoble quality. And yet Christianity sets it in the very forefront of the Christian virtues; it is indeed the virtue on which all the other virtues depend and from which they come. Whence then comes this Christian humility, and what does it involve?

(*a*) Christian humility comes from *self-knowledge*. Bernard said of it, " It is the virtue by which a man becomes conscious of his own unworthiness, in consequence of the truest knowledge of himself." To face oneself is the most humiliating thing in the world. Most of us dramatize ourselves; most of us see ourselves as the centre of some dramatic action in life. Somewhere there is a story of a man who before he went to sleep at night dreamed his waking dreams. He would see himself as the hero of some thrilling rescue from the sea or from the flames; he would see himself as an orator holding a vast audience spellbound; he would see himself walking to the wicket in a Test Match at Lord's and scoring a century; he would see himself in some international football match dazzling the crowd with his skill; always he was the centre of the picture. Most of us are essentially like that. And true humility comes when we face ourselves, when we see our own weakness, our own selfishness, our own failure in work and in personal relationships and in achievement. Humility depends on honesty; it depends on having the courage to look at ourselves without the rose-tinted spectacles of self-dramatization, and self-admiration, and self-love.

(*b*) Christian humility comes from *setting life beside the life of Christ and in the light of the demands of God*. God is perfection, and to satisfy perfection is not difficult, it is impossible. The fact that we are men means that we are always engaged on a hopeless task. So long as we compare ourselve with second bests, we may come out of the comparison well. It is when we compare ourselves with perfection that we see our own failure. A girl may think herself a very fine pianist—until she has heard Myra Hess or Eileen Joyce or Solomon or Kentner. A man may think himself a good golfer until he has seen Hogan and Snead and Cotton. A man may think himself something of a scholar until he picks up one of the books of the great old scholars with their encyclopaedic knowledge. A man may think himself a fine preacher until he hears one of the princes of the pulpit. Self-satisfaction depends on the standard with which we compare ourselves. If we compare ourselves with our neighbour and with the man or the woman next door, we shall probably emerge very satisfactorily from the comparison. But the Christian standard

is Jesus Christ and the demands of the perfection of God—
and against that standard there is no room for pride.

(c) There is another way of putting this. R. C. Trench
said that humility comes from the constant sense of our
own *creatureliness*. We are God's creatures, God's creation.
We are in absolute dependence on God. As the hymn
has it:

> " 'Tis Thou preservest me from death
>   And dangers every hour;
> I cannot draw another breath
>   Unless Thou give me power.
>
> My health, my friends, and parents dear
>   To me by God are given;
> I have not any blessing here
>   But what is sent from heaven."

Of ourselves we have nothing. We can never give; we
must always take. We are creatures, and for the creature
there can be nothing but humility in the presence of the
creator.

The Christian humility is based on the sight of self, the
vision of Christ, and the realization of God.

THE CHRISTIAN GENTLEMAN

Ephesians 4: 1-3 (*continued*)

(ii) THE second of the great Christian virtues is what the
Authorized Version calls *meekness*, and what we have
translated *gentleness*. The Greek noun is *praotēs* and the
adjective is *praus*, and these are words beyond translation
by any single word. Let us see what this virtue means and
involves. In Greek *praus* has two main lines of meanings.

(*a*) Aristotle, the great Greek thinker and teacher, has
much to say about *praotēs*. It was Aristotle's custom to
define every virtue as the *mean between two extremes*.

On the one side there was excess of some quality, on the other there was defect; and in between there was the quality in exactly its right proportion in life. Now Aristotle defines *praotēs* as the mean between excessive anger and excessive angerlessness; it is the mean between being too angry and never being angry at all. The man who is *praus* is the man who is always angry at the right time and never angry at the wrong time. To put that in another way, the man who is *praus* is the man who is kindled by indignation at the wrongs and the sufferings of others, but who is never moved to anger by the wrongs and the insults he himself has to bear. So, then, the man who is (as in the Authorized Version), *meek* is the man who is always angry at the right time, but who is never angry at the wrong time.

(b) But there is another fact which will illumine the meaning of this word. *Praus* is the Greek word for an animal which has been trained to obey the reins or the word of command, an animal which has been trained and domesticated until it is completely under discipline and under control. Therefore the man who is *meek*, *praus*, is the man who has every instinct and every passion, every motion of his mind and heart and tongue and desire, under perfect control. It would not be right to say that such a man is entirely and completely self-controlled, for such self-control is beyond human power; but it would be right to say that such a man is God-controlled. He is the man on the tiller of whose life is the hand of God.

Here then is the second great Christian virtue, the second great characteristic of the true member of the Church. He is the man who is so God-controlled that he is always angry at the right time, but never angry at the wrong time; he is a man in whom self has died and whose whole life is directed and controlled by God. He is God's gentleman.

THE UNDEFEATABLE PATIENCE

Ephesians 4: 1-3 *(continued)*

(iii) THE third great quality of the Christian is what the Authorized Version calls *long-suffering*. The Greek word is *makrothumia*. This word has two main directions of meaning.

(*a*) It describes the spirit which will never give in, and which, because it endures to the end, will reap the promise and the reward. Its meaning can best be seen from the fact that a Jewish writer used it to describe what he called " the Roman persistency which would never make peace under defeat." In their great days the Romans were unconquerable; they might lose a battle; they might even lose a campaign, but they could not conceive of losing a war. In the greatest and the most shattering disaster it never occurred to them to give in and to admit defeat. The Christian patience is the spirit which never admits defeat, which will not be defeated by any task, which will not be broken by any misfortune or suffering, which will not be deterred by any disappointment or discouragement, but which persists and endures to the end.

(*b*) But *makrothumia*, *patience*, *long-suffering* has in Greek an even more characteristic meaning than that. It is the characteristic Greek word for *patience with men*. Chrysostom defined it as the spirit which has the power to take revenge, but which never does so. Lightfoot defined it as the spirit which refuses to retaliate. It is the spirit which bears with everything which men can do to it. To take a very imperfect analogy—it is often possible to see a puppy and a very large dog together. The puppy yaps at the big dog; he worries him; he bites him; he growls at him; he attacks him; and all the time the big dog, who could annihilate the puppy with one snap of his teeth, bears the puppy's impertinence with a grave and forbearing dignity. *Makrothumia*, *patience*, *long-suffering* is the spirit which bears insult and injury

163

without bitterness and without complaint. It is the spirit which bears the sheer foolishness of men without irritation. It is the spirit which can suffer unpleasant people with graciousness and fools without complaint.

The thing which best of all gives its meaning is that the New Testament repeatedly uses it of God. Paul asks the impenitent sinner: " Do you despise the *long-suffering* of God? " (*Romans* 2: 4). Paul speaks of the *long-suffering* of Jesus to him (I *Timothy* I: 16). Christ had had patience with Paul the persecutor. Peter speaks of the *long-suffering* of God waiting in the days of Noah (I *Peter* 3: 20). He says that the *long-suffering* of God is our salvation (2 *Peter* 3: 15). If God had been a man, He would long since have taken His hand and in sheer irritation wiped the world out for all its disobedience. But God's patience waits and loves. The Christian must have the patience towards his fellow men which God has shown to him.

THE CHRISTIAN LOVE

Ephesians 4: 1-3 (*continued*)

(iv) The fourth great Christian quality is the quality of *love*. Christian love was something so new that the Christian writers had to invent a new word for it; or, at least, they had to take a word which was a very unusual Greek word. It is the word *agapē*. In Greek there are four words for *love*. There is *erōs*, which is the love between a man and a maid, and which definitely involves sexual passion. There is *philia* which is the warm affection which exists between those who are very near and very dear to each other. There is *storgē* which is characteristically the word for family affection. And there is this word *agapē*, which the Authorized Version translates sometimes *love* and sometimes *charity*. The real meaning of *agapē* is unconquerable benevolence. If we regard a person with *agapē*, it means that nothing that that person can or will ever do will make us seek anything but his highest good. Though he injure us and hurt us and insult us, we will never feel anything but kindness towards him. That quite clearly means one thing. It means that this Christian *agapē, love,* is not an emotional thing. We talk about falling in love; and love to our nearest and dearest is something which we cannot help. But this Christian *agapē* is a thing, not only of the emotions, but also of the will. It is a conquest. It is the ability to retain this unconquerable good will to the unlovely and the unlovable, and towards those who do not love us. As someone has put it, *agapē* is the power to love even the people whom we do not like. *Agapē* is that quality of mind and heart which compels a Christian never to feel any bitterness, never to feel any desire for revenge, but always to seek nothing but the highest good of every man no matter what men do to him.

(v) So then we have the four great virtues of the Christian life—humility, gentleness, patience, love. And these four issue in a fifth, and that fifth is *peace.* It is Paul's advice and urgent request that the people to whom he is writing should eagerly preserve " the sacred oneness " which should characterize the true Church. Peace may be defined as *right relationships between man and man.* This oneness, this peace, these right relationships can only be preserved in one way. Every one of the four great Christian virtues depends on one thing—on the obliteration of self. So long as self is at the centre of things, so long as our feelings, our prestige, are the only things that matter, this oneness can never fully exist. It can only exist when we cease to make self the centre of things and when we think more of others than we do of ourselves. Self kills peace. In a society where self predominates, men cannot be other than a disintegrated collection of individualistic and warring units. But when self dies and Christ springs to life within our hearts, then there comes the peace, the oneness, the togetherness, which is the great hall-mark of the true Church.

THE BASIS OF UNITY

Ephesians 4: 4-6

> There is one body and one Spirit, just as you have been called with one hope of your calling. There is one Lord, one faith, one baptism, one God and Father of all, who is above all, and through all, and in all.

Now Paul goes on to set down the basis on which the Christian unity is founded.

(i) There is one body. Christ is the head and the Church is the body. No brain can work through a body which is disintegrated and unco-ordinated and split into fragments. Unless there is a co-ordinated oneness in the body, the thoughts and plans and designs of the head and the brain are hindered and frustrated. The oneness of the Church is essential for the work of Christ. That does not need to be a mechanical oneness of administration and of human organization; but it does need to be a oneness founded on a common love of Christ and of every part for the other.

(ii) There is one Spirit. The word *pneuma* in Greek means both *spirit* and *breath*; it is in fact the usual and ordinary word for breath. Unless the breath be in the body, the body is dead; and the vitalizing breath of the body of the Church is the Spirit of Christ. It is the operation of the Spirit in the body which gives the body life and which keeps it alive. There can be no Church without the Spirit; and there can be no receiving of the Spirit without silent and prayerful waiting for Him.

(iii) There is one hope in our calling. We are all proceeding towards the same goal. Herein is the great secret of unity. Our methods may be different, our organization may be different, even some of our beliefs may be different; but we are all striving towards the one goal, the goal of a world redeemed in Christ.

(iv) There is one Lord. The nearest approach to a creed which the early Church possessed was the short sentence: " Jesus Christ is Lord " (*Philippians* 2: 11). As Paul saw it, it was the dream of God that there should come a day when all men confessed that " Jesus Christ is Lord." The word used for Lord is the word *kurios*. It has two usages in ordinary Greek which show us something of what Paul meant. It is the word which is used for *master* in contradistinction to *servant* or *slave*; and it was the regular designation of the Roman Emperor. Christians are joined together because they are all in the possession and in the service of the one Master and the one King.

(v) There is one faith. By this Paul did not mean that there is one *creed*. It is very seldom indeed that the word *faith* means a *creed* in the New Testament. By faith the New Testament nearly always means the complete trust and surrender of the Christian in and to Jesus Christ. What Paul means is that all Christians are bound together in one because all of them have made one common act of complete surrender to the love of Jesus Christ. It may well be that they describe their act of surrender in different terms in different creeds; but however they describe it, that act of surrender is the one thing which is common to all of them.

(vi) There is one baptism. There is one gateway to the Christian Church. In the early Church baptism was usually adult baptism, because men and women were coming direct from heathenism into the Christian Church. And, therefore, before anything else, baptism was a public confession of faith. There was only one way for a Roman soldier to join the army; he had to take the oath that he would be true for ever to his emperor and his king. There was only one way to enter the Christian Church— the way of public confession of Jesus Christ.

(vii) There is one God. Now see what Paul says about the God in whom we believe. He is the *Father* of all; in that phrase the *love* of God is for ever enshrined. The greatest thing, the unique thing about the Christian God, is not that He is King, not that He is Judge, but that He is

Father. The Christian idea of God begins in love. He is *above* all; in that phrase is enshrined the *control* of God. No matter what things may look like God is in control. There may be floods; but " The Lord sitteth on the flood " (*Psalm* 29: 10) as the Psalmist said. Nothing is outwith the control of God. He is *through* all; in that phrase is enshrined the *providence* of God. God did not create the world and set it going, as a man might wind up a clockwork toy and leave it to run down. God is all through His world, guiding, directing, sustaining, upholding, loving. In everything and through everything the providence of God is active and operative and powerful. He is *in* all; that phrase enshrines the *presence* of God in all life. It may be that Paul took the germ of this idea from the Stoics. The Stoics believed that God was a fire, purer than any earthly fire, fiery spirit at its clearest and its purest. And they believed that what gave a man life was that a spark of that fire which was God came and dwelt within his body. It was Paul's belief that in everything there is God. In man and in the mind of man, in the world and in all growing things, in history and in events, in everything there is God. It is the Christian belief that we live in a God-created, God-controlled, God-sustained, God-filled world.

THE GIFTS OF GRACE

Ephesians 4: 7-10

> To each one of you grace has been given, as it has been measured out to you by the free gift of Christ. There- fore scripture says, " He ascended into the height and brought His captive band of prisoners, and gave gifts to men." (When it says that " He ascended," what else can it mean than that He also descended into the lower parts of the earth? He who descended is the same person as He who ascended above all the heavens, that He might fill all things with His presence.

Now Paul turns to another aspect of his subject. He has been talking about the *qualities* of the members of Christ's Church; now he is going to talk of their *functions* in the Church. He is going to talk about how they can best use their abilities and their talents and their gifts in the service of the Church; and he begins by laying down what was for him an essential truth—the fact that every gift a man has is the gift of the grace of Christ. He is thinking of Jesus as the giver of all the gifts which the Christian possesses.

> " And every virtue we possess,
>> And every victory won,
> And every thought of holiness,
>> Are His alone."

To make his point about Christ the giver of gifts, Paul quotes a verse from the Psalms. He quotes this verse with a very significant difference. It is a verse from *Psalm 68*. This Psalm describes a king's conquering return. The conquering king ascends on high; that is to say, he climbs the steep road of Mount Zion into the streets of the Holy City. He brings in his captive band of prisoners. That is to say, he marches in triumph through the streets with his prisoners in chains behind him to demonstrate his conquering power. And now there comes the difference. The verse in the Psalm is, " Thou hast ascended on high; thou hast led captive captivity; thou hast received gifts for men; yea for the rebellious also, that the Lord God might dwell among them " (*Psalm* 68: 18). The conqueror has come home with his trophies; and he demands the ransom and the tribute that the peoples he has conquered must give to him. Now see the change that Paul makes: " He ascended into the height, and brought His captive band of prisoners, and *gave* gifts to men." In the Old Testament the conquering king *demanded and received* gifts from men: in the New Testament the conqueror Christ *offers and gives* gifts to men. That is the essential difference between the two Testaments. In the Old

Testament God is a God who demands; in the New Testament God is a God who gives. In the Old Testament a jealous God demands and insists on tribute from men; in the New Testament a loving God pours out His love to men and gives them all He has to give. That indeed is the message of the good news.

Then, as so often, Paul's mind goes off at a word. He has used the word *ascended*, and that makes him think of Jesus. And it makes him say a very wonderful thing. Jesus *descended* into this world when He entered it as a man; Jesus *ascended* from this world when He left it to return to His glory. Paul's great thought is that the Christ who ascended and the Christ who descended are one and the same person. What does that mean? It means that the Christ of glory is the same as the Jesus who trod this earth; still He loves all men; still He seeks the sinner; still He heals the sufferer; still He comforts the sorrowing; still He is the friend of outcast men and women. It is Paul's most precious thought that even in His glory Christ has never forgotten His love. As the Scottish paraphrase has it:

> " Though now ascended up on high,
> He bends on earth a brother's eye;
> Partaker of the human name,
> He knows the frailty of our frame.
>
> Our fellow suff'rer yet retains
> A fellow-feeling of our pains;
> And still remembers in the skies
> His tears, His agonies and cries.
>
> In every pang that rends the heart
> The Man of sorrows has a part;
> He sympathizes with our grief,
> And to the suff'rer sends relief."

The ascended Christ is still the lover of the souls of men.

And then still another thought strikes Paul. Jesus ascended up on high. But He did not ascend up on high to leave the world; He ascended up on high to fill the world

170

with His presence. When Jesus was here in this world in the flesh, He could only be in one place at one time; He was under all the limitations of the body; but when He laid this body aside and when He returned to glory, He was liberated from the limitations of the body and He was able to be everywhere in all the world through His Spirit. To Paul the ascension of Jesus meant not a Christ-deserted, but a Christ-filled world.

THE OFFICE-BEARERS OF THE CHURCH

Ephesians 4: 11-13

> And He gave to the Church some as apostles, and some as prophets, and some as evangelists, and some as pastors and teachers. This He did that God's consecrated people should be fully equipped, that the work of service might go on, and that the body of Christ should be built up. And this is to go on until we all arrive at complete unity in faith in and knowledge of God, until we reach perfect manhood, until we reach a stature which can be measured by the fullness of Christ.

THERE is a special interest in this passage because it gives us a picture of the organization and the administration of the early Church. It gives us a list of the office-bearers of the Church in the time of Paul. In the early Church there were three kinds of office-bearers. There were a few whose writ and whose authority ran throughout the whole Church. There were many whose ministry was not confined to one place, but who carried out a wandering ministry, going wherever the Spirit moved them, and where God sent them. There were some whose ministry was a local ministry which was confined to the one congregation and to the one place.

(i) The *apostles* were those whose authority ran throughout the whole Church. The apostles included more than the Twelve. Barnabas was an apostle (*Acts* 14: 4, 17). James the brother of our Lord, was an apostle (I *Corinthians* 15: 17; *Galatians* I: 19). Silvanus was an apostle (I *Thessalonians* 2: 6). Andronicus and Junia were apostles (*Romans* 16: 7). But for an apostle there were two great qualifications. First, an apostle must have seen Jesus. When Paul is claiming his own rights in face of the opposition of Corinth, he demands: " Am I not an apostle? Have I not seen Jesus Christ our Lord? " (I *Corinthians* 9: I). Second, an apostle had to be a witness of the Resurrection and of the Risen Lord. When the eleven met to elect a successor to Judas, the traitor, the qualification of the successor was that he must be one of those who had companied with them throughout the earthly life of Jesus, and that he must be ordained to be a witness to the Resurrection (*Acts* I: 21, 22). In a sense the apostles were bound to die out, because before so very long those who had actually seen Jesus, and who had actually witnessed the Resurrection, would pass from this world. But in another sense, and in a still greater sense, the qualification still remains. He who would teach Christ must still know Christ; and he who would bring the power of Christ to others must still have experienced Christ's risen power.

(ii) There were the *prophets*. The word prophet does not so much mean a *fore-teller* as a *forth-teller*. The prophets did not so much *fore-tell* the future as *forth-tell* the will of God. In forth-telling the will of God, they necessarily to some extent fore-told the future, because they announced to men the consequences which would follow if men disobeyed that will. The prophets were wanderers throughout the Church. Their message was held to be not the result of thought and study, but the direct result of the Holy Spirit. They had no homes and no families and no means of support. They went from Church to Church proclaiming the will of God as God had told it to them. The prophets before long vanished from the Church. There were three reasons why the prophets vanished from the scene. (*a*) In times of persecution the prophets were the first to suffer; their occupation was a dangerous occupation; they had no means of concealment; they were the first to die for the faith. (*b*) The prophets became a problem. As the Church grew the local organization developed. Each congregation began to grow into an organization which had its own permanent minister and its own local administration. Before so very long the settled ministry began to resent the intrusion of these wandering prophets, who often disturbed their congregations. The settled ministry always tends to resent the itinerant evangelist. The inevitable result was that bit by bit the prophets faded out, and the settled ministry was supreme. (*c*) The office of prophet was singularly liable to abuse. These prophetic wanderers had a very considerable prestige. Some of them abused their office and made it an excuse for living a very comfortable life at the expense of the congregations whom they visited. The earliest book of church administration is the *Didachē*, *The Teaching of the Twelve Apostles*, which dates back to just after A.D. 100. In it both the prestige and the suspicion of the prophets is clearly seen. The order for sacrament is given, and the prayers to be used are set out, and then there comes the instruction that the prophet is to be allowed to celebrate the sacrament as he will. He is not to be bound by the ordinary forms if he wishes to take his own way of it. But there are also certain other regulations. It is laid down that a wandering prophet may stay one or two days with a congregation, but if he wishes to stay three days he is a false prophet; it is laid down that if any wandering prophet in a moment of alleged inspiration demands money or a meal, he is a false prophet. There were days when the prophets were the real messengers of God to the Church and it was so in the day of Paul. But the time came when these wandering prophets were an anachronism, and when some of them brought discredit on their office, and in the end they vanished from the scene.

(iii) There were the *evangelists*. The evangelists too were wanderers. They corresponded to what we would call missionaries. Paul writes to Timothy, " Do the work of an evangelist " (2 *Timothy* 4: 5). They were the bringers of the good news. They had not the prestige and authority of the apostles who had seen the Lord; they had not the influence of the Spirit-inspired prophets; they were the rank and file missionaries of the Church who took the story of the good news to a world which had never heard it. These anonymous evangelists are dismissed in the New Testament story with little more than a mention; but they must have been the nameless servants who took the name of Christ to all the world.

(iv) There were *the pastors and teachers*. It would seem that this double phrase describes one set of people. They were *teachers*. In one sense they had the most important task in the whole Church; they were not wanderers; they were settled and permanent in the work of one congregation. They had a triple function. (*a*) It has to be remembered that in the early Church there were very few books. Printing was not to be invented for almost another fourteen hundred years. Every book had to be written by hand and a book the size of the New Testament would cost as much as £40. That meant that the story of Jesus had to be transmitted by word of mouth. The story of Jesus was told long before it was written down; and these teachers had the tremendous responsibility of being the repositories of the gospel story. It was their function to know and to pass on the story of the life of Jesus. It is to them that we owe the fact that the story of Jesus came down in the Church. (*b*) The people who came into the Church were coming straight from heathenism; they knew literally nothing about Christianity, except that Jesus Christ had laid hold upon their hearts. Therefore these teachers had to teach and open out the Christian faith to the converts who came into the Church from the heathen world. They had to teach and to explain the great doctrines of the Christian faith. It was in their hands that the purity of doctrine lay. It is to them that we owe it that the Christian faith remained pure and was not distorted as it was handed down. (c) These teachers were also *pastors* and the word *pastor* is simply the Latin word for a *shepherd*. At this time the Christian Church was no more than a little island in a sea of paganism. The people who came into it were only one remove from their heathen lives; they were constantly open to the infection of the heathen world; they were in constant danger of relapsing into heathenism. And the duty of the pastor was to shepherd his flock and to keep them safe. The word is an ancient and an honourable word. As far back as Homeric times Agamemnon the king was called the Shepherd of the People. Jesus had called Himself the Good Shepherd (*John* 10: 11, 14). The writer to the Hebrews called Jesus the great shepherd of the sheep (*Hebrews* 13: 20). Peter called Jesus the shepherd of men's souls (I *Peter* 2: 25). He called Him the Chief Shepherd (I *Peter* 5: 4). It had been Jesus' command to Peter that Peter should feed His sheep (*John* 21: 16). Paul had warned the elders of Ephesus that they must guard the flock whom God had committed to their care (*Acts* 20: 28). Peter had exhorted the elders to feed the flock of God (I *Peter* 5: 2). The picture of the shepherd is indelibly written on the New Testament. The shepherd was the man who cared for the flock and led the sheep into safe places; he was the man who sought the sheep when they wandered away and who brought them back again; he was the man who defended the sheep from their enemies and, if need be, died to save them. The shepherd of the flock of God is the man who bears God's people on his heart, who feeds them with the truth, who seeks them when they stray away, and who defends them from all that would hurt or destroy or distort their faith. And this is no official office; it is the duty that is laid on every Christian that he should be a shepherd to all his brethren.

K—7

THE AIM OF THE OFFICE-BEARER

Ephesians 4: 11-13 (*continued*)

AFTER Paul has named the different kinds of office-bearers within the Church, he goes on to speak of the aim of the office-bearers and of what they must try to do.

Their aim is that the members of the Church should be fully equipped. The word which Paul uses for *equipped* is an interesting word. It is the word *katartismon* which comes from the verb *katartizein*. The word is used in surgery for setting a broken limb, or for putting a joint that is out of place back into its place. In politics it is used for bringing together opposing factions so that government can go on. In the New Testament itself it is used of mending nets (*Mark* 1: 19), and of disciplining an offender until he is fit to take his place again within the fellowship of the Church (*Galatians* 6: 1). The basic idea of the word is that of putting a thing or a person into the condition in which he or it ought to be. It is the function of the office-bearers of the Church to see that the members of the Church are so educated, so helped, so guided, so cared for, so sought out when they go astray, that they become what they ought to be. The office-bearer of the Church holds his office, not for his own honour, but for the help he can give his fellow-members within the Church.

Their aim is that the work of service may go on. The word used for service is *diakonia*, and the main idea which lies behind this word is that of *practical service*. The work of the Church lies not only in preaching and teaching, but in practical service. The office-bearer is not to be a man who simply talks and argues on matters of theology and of Church law. He is in office to see that practical service of God's poor and lonely people goes on.

Their aim is to see to it that the body of Christ is built up. Always the work of the office-bearer is construction, and not destruction. His aim is always the building up, and never the disruption, of the Church. His aim is never to make trouble, but always to see that trouble does not rear its head. His aim is always to strengthen, and never to loosen, the fabric of the Church.

But the office-bearer has even greater aims than these. These may be said to be his immediate and day to day aims. But beyond that he has still greater aims.

His aim is that the members of the Church should arrive at perfect unity. He must never allow parties to form within the Church; he must never do anything which would cause differences within the Church. His aim must be by precept and example to draw the members of the Church into a closer unity every day.

His aim is that the members of the Church should reach perfect manhood. The aim of the Church for its members is nothing less than perfection. The Church can never be content that her members should live decent, respectable lives; her aim must be that they should be examples of perfect Christian manhood and womanhood.

And so Paul ends with an aim than which none could be greater. The aim of the Church is that her members should reach a stature which can be measured by the fullness of Christ. In a daring phrase, A. J. Gossip used to say that Christ's aim was to produce in this world a race of Christs. The aim of the Church is nothing less than to produce men and women who have in them the reflection of Jesus Christ Himself. It is told that during the Crimean War Florence Nightingale was passing one night down a hospital ward. She paused to bend over the bed of a sorely wounded soldier. As she looked down, the wounded lad looked up and said: " You're Christ to me." A saint has been defined as " someone in whom Christ lives again." And that is what the true Church member ought to be.

GROWING INTO CHRIST

Ephesians 4: 14-16

All this must be done so that we should no longer be
infants in the faith, wave-tossed and blown hither and
thither by every wind of teaching, by the clever
trickery of men, by cunning cleverness designed to
make us take a wandering way. Instead of that it
is all designed to make us cherish the truth in love,
and to make us grow in all things into Him who is
the head—it is Christ I mean. It is from Christ that
the whole body is fitted and united together, by means
of all the joints which supply its needs, according
as each part performs the share of the task allotted
to it. It is from Him that the body grows and builds
itself up in love.

IN every Church there are certain members who must
be protected. There are those who are like children;
they are dominated by a desire for novelty; they are at
the mercy of the latest fashion in religion; they are always
under the influence of the last person to whom they talked;
they have a childish inability to concentrate on the essentials
of the faith. It is the lesson of history that popular fashions
in religion come and go, but the Church continues for
ever. It is the lesson of history that itinerant teachers
and evangelists rise and fall, but the Church continues
to go on. The solid food of religion is always to be found
within the Church.

In every Church there are certain people who have to be
guarded against. Paul speaks of the clever trickery of
men; the word he uses (*kubeia*) means skill in manipulating
the dice. There are always those who by clever and ingenious
arguments seek to lure people away from their faith.
It is one of the characteristics of our age that people
talk about religion more to-day than they have done
for many years; and the Christian, especially the young
Christian, has often to meet the clever arguments of those
who are against the Church and against God.

There is only one way to avoid being blown about by the
latest religious fashion, and to avoid being seduced by the

specious arguments of clever men, and that is by continual growth into Christ, by living nearer and closer to Him every day.

Paul uses still another picture. He says that a body is only healthy and fit and efficient when every part in it is thoroughly integrated and co-ordinated, when every joint is doing its connecting work, when every part of the body is playing the part in the work of the body that is allotted to it. Paul says that the Church is like that; and the Church can only be like that when Christ is really the head, and when every member in it is moving under the control of Christ, just as every part of a healthy body moves at the behest of the brain.

The only thing which can keep the individual Christian solid in the faith and secure against all seduction, the only thing which can keep the whole Church healthy and efficient, is an intimate and indissoluble connection with Jesus Christ who is the head and the directing mind of the whole body.

THE THINGS WHICH MUST BE ABANDONED

Ephesians 4: 17-24

> I say this and I solemnly lay it upon you in the Lord—
> you must no longer live the kind of life the Gentiles
> live, for their minds are concerned with empty things;
> their understandings are darkened; they are strangers
> from the life God gives, because of the ignorance that is
> in them and because of the petrifying of their hearts.
> They have come to a stage when they are past feeling;
> and in their shameless wantonness they have aban-
> doned themselves to every kind of unclean conduct
> in the insatiable lust of their desires. But that is not
> the way that you have learned Christ, if indeed you
> have really listened to Him, and have been taught in
> Him, as the true teaching in Jesus is. You must stop
> living in your former way of life. You must put off
> your old manhood, which is perishing, as deceitful
> desires are bound to make it do. You must be renewed

in the spirit of your minds. You must put on the new manhood, created after God's pattern, in righteousness and in true holiness.

HERE is Paul's appeal to his converts to leave their old way of life, and to turn to Christ's way of life. In this passage Paul picks out what he considers the essential characteristics of heathen life to be. The heathen are concerned with empty things which do not matter; their minds are darkened because of their ignorance. And then comes the salient word; their hearts are *petrified*. The word which Paul uses for the *petrifying* of their hearts is a grim and terrible word. It is the word *pōrōsis*. *Pōrōsis* comes from a word *pōros*, which originally meant a stone that was harder than marble. It came to have certain medical uses. It was used for the chalk stone which can form in the joints and completely paralyse action. It is used of the callus that forms where a bone has been broken and has been re-set, a callus which is harder than the bone itself. Finally the word comes to mean the loss of all power of sensation. It describes something which has become so hardened, so petrified that it has no power to feel at all. That is what Paul says the heathen life is like. It is a life which has become so hardened that it has lost the power of feeling. In the *Epistle to a Young Friend*, Robert Burns wrote about sin:

> " I waive the quantum o' the sin,
>   The hazard of concealing;
> But och! it hardens a' within,
>   And petrifies the feeling! "

The terror of sin is its petrifying effect. The process of sin is quite discernible. No man becomes a great sinner all at once. At first he regards sin with fear and horror. When he sins, there enters into his heart remorse and regret. But if he continues to sin there comes a time when he loses all sensation, when he can do the most shameful things without any feeling at all. His conscience is petrified. It was Paul's great accusation that a heathen way of life petrifies a man's conscience, until there is no feeling left in it at all.

But Paul uses two other terrible Greek words to describe the heathen way of life. He says that they have abandoned themselves to every kind of unclean conduct in *the insatiable lust of their desires*. And he says they have done so in their *shameless wantonness*. The word for shameless wantonness is *aselgeia*. It is defined by Plato as " impudence "; it is defined by another writer as " preparedness for every pleasure." It is defined by Basil as " a disposition of the soul incapable of bearing the pain of discipline." But the great characteristic of *aselgeia* is this—the bad man usually tries to hide his sin; but the man who has *aselgeia* in his soul does not care how much he shocks public opinion, how much he defies and insults all decency so long as he can gratify his desires. Most men have enough decency left to seek to hide their sins; but the man in whom there is *aselgeia* does not care who sees his shame so long as he gets what he wants. Sin can get such a grip of a man that he is lost to decency and shame. He is like a drug taker. At first he takes the drug in secret; but he can come to a stage when he will shamelessly and openly plead and even grovel and whine for the drug on which he has become dependent. A man can become such a slave of liquor that he does not care who sees him drunk. A man can let his sexual desires so master him that he does not care who sees him satisfy them. The heathen way of life can become so mastered and dominated by sin that it loses even natural shame, so that a man ceases to be a man, and reverts to being a beast.

The Christless man does all this in the *insatiable lust of his desires*. The word is *pleonexia*, and it is another terrible word. The Greeks defined it as " arrogant greediness." They defined it as " the accursed love of possessing." They defined it as " the unlawful desire for the things which belong to others." It has been defined as the spirit in which a man is always ready to sacrifice his neighbour to his own desires. *Pleonexia* is the irresistible desire to have what we have no right to have. It might issue in the theft of material things; it might issue in the spirit which tramples on other people to get its own way; it might issue in sexual sin. It is the spirit of the man who does not care whom he hurts and what method he uses so long as he gets what he desires.

In the heathen world, the Christless world, Paul saw three terrible things. He saw men's hearts so petrified that they were not even aware that they were sinning; he saw men so dominated by sin that shame was lost and decency forgotten; he saw men so much at the mercy of their desires that they did not care whose life they injured and whose innocence they destroyed so long as these desires were satisfied. When we think of it, these are exactly the sins of the Christless world to-day, the sins that can be seen invading life at every point and stalking the streets of every great city.

Paul urges his converts to have done with that kind of life. He uses a vivid way of speaking. He says: " Put off your old way of life as you would put off an old suit of clothes; clothe yourself in a new way; put off your sins, and put on the righteousness and the holiness which God can give you." There are few passages which so show the terrible ugliness of sin, and which so urge a man to abandon the world's way, and to take God's way of things.

THINGS WHICH MUST BE BANISHED FROM LIFE

Ephesians 4: 25-32

So then strip yourselves of falsehood, and let each of you speak the truth with his neighbour, because we are all members of the same body. Be angry—but be angry in such a way that your anger is not a sin. Do not let the sun set on your wrath, and do not give the devil any opportunity. Let him who was a thief steal no more; rather let him take to hard work, and to producing good with his hands, in order that he may be able to share with the man who is in need. Do not allow any foul word to issue from your mouth; but let your words be good, designed for necessary edification, that they may bring benefit to those who hear them. Do not grieve the Holy Spirit of God, with whom you are sealed until the day of your redemption comes. Let all bitterness, all outbreaks of passion, all long-lived anger, all loud talking, all insulting language be removed from you with all evil. Show yourselves kind to one another, merciful, forgiving one another, as God in Christ forgave you.

PAUL has just been saying that when a man becomes a Christian, he must put off his old life as a man puts off a coat for which he has no further use. Here Paul speaks of the things which must be banished from the Christian life.

(i) There must be no more falsehood. There is more than one kind of lie in this world. There is the lie in speech and in words. Sometimes that lie is deliberate and sometimes it is almost unconscious. Dr. Johnson has an interesting bit of advice in regard to the bringing up of children. He says: " Accustom your children constantly to this (the telling of the truth); if a thing happened at one window, and they, when relating it, say that it happened at another, do not let it pass, but instantly check them; you do not know where deviation from truth will end. . . . It is more from carelessness about truth than from intentional lying, that there is so much falsehood in the world." It was Dr. Johnson's view that we must accustom ourselves to make a deliberate resolve and attempt to tell the truth. It is easy to embroider the details of a story. It is easy to make up some sort of story when we are making an excuse for not doing, or for not having done, something. It is perfectly true that there is a great deal of almost unconscious falsehood in the world, and that truth demands a deliberate effort. But there is not only the lie of speech; there is also the lie of silence, and maybe it is even commoner yet. André Maurois, in a memorable phrase, speaks of " the menace of things unsaid." It may be that in some discussion a man keeps silent when he should have spoken, and by his silence gives approval to some course of action which he knows is wrong. It may be that a man withholds warning and rebuke when he knows quite well he should have given it. A man can stifle the truth by silence, just as much as he can twist it by words.

Then Paul gives the reason for telling the truth. It is because we are all members of the same body. We can only live in safety because the senses and the nerves pass true messages to the brain. If in fact the senses and the nerves took to passing false messages to the brain, if, for instance, they told the brain that something was cool and touchable when in fact it was hot and burning, life would very soon come to an end. A body can only function accurately and healthily when each part of it passes true messages to the brain and to the other parts. If then we are all bound into one body, that body can only function when we speak the truth. All deception impairs the working of the body of Christ.

(ii) There must be anger in the Christian life, but it must be the right kind of anger. There would be something essential missing in a man who had lost the faculty of being angry. Selfish anger, anger at what happens to oneself, is always wrong. Crossness and bad temper and irritability are without defence. But there is an anger without which the world would be a poorer place. The world would have lost much without the blazing anger of Wilberforce against the slave trade, and of Shaftesbury against the conditions in which men, women and children worked in the nineteenth century. There was a certain rugged bluntness about Dr. Johnson. When he thought a thing was wrong, he said so and said so with force and directness When he was about to publish the *Tour to the Hebrides*, Hannah More asked him, as she said, to mitigate some of its asperities. She tells that his answer was that " he would not cut off his claws, nor make his tiger a cat, to please anybody." There is a place for the tiger in life;

and when the tiger becomes a tabby cat, something goes lost. There were times when Jesus was terribly and majestically angry. He was angry when the scribes and Pharisees were watching to see if He would heal the man with the withered hand on the Sabbath day (*Mark* 3: 5). It was not their criticism of Himself at which He was angry; He was angry that their rigid orthodoxy desired to impose unnecessary suffering on a fellow creature. He was angry when He made a whip and drove the changers of money and the sellers of victims from the Temple courts (*John* 2: 13-17). F. W. Boreham tells how F. W. Robertson of Brighton, that great preacher and saint, tells in one of his letters, that he bit his lips until they bled when he met on the street a certain man whom he knew to be luring a pure young girl to her destruction. There was white hot anger in Robertson's heart. John Wesley said: " Give me a hundred men who fear nothing but God, and *who hate nothing but sin*, and who know nothing but Jesus Christ and Him crucified, and I will shake the world." The anger which is selfish, passionate, undisciplined, uncontrolled is a sinful, a useless and a hurtful thing, which must be banished from the Christian life. But the anger which is disciplined into the service of Christ and of our fellow men, and which is utterly pure and utterly selfless, is one of the great dynamic forces in this world.

THINGS WHICH MUST BE BANISHED FROM LIFE

Ephesians 4: 25-32 (*continued*)

(iii) PAUL goes on to say that the Christian must never let the sun set upon his wrath. Plutarch tells us that the disciples of Pythagoras, the philosopher, had a rule of their society, that if, during the day, anger had made them speak insultingly to each other, before the sun set they shook hands and kissed each other, and were reconciled. There was a Jewish Rabbi whose prayer it was that he might never go to sleep with any bitter thought against a brother man within his mind. No man could hope to come to the end of the day better than at peace with all men. Paul's advice is sound, because the longer we postpone mending a quarrel and a breach, the less likely we are ever to mend it. If there is trouble between us and anyone else, if there is trouble in a Church or a fellowship or any society where men meet, the only way to deal with it is at once. The longer it is left to flourish, the more bitter and inveterate it will grow. If we have been in the wrong, we must pray to God to give us grace to go and admit that it was so; and even if we have been right, we must pray to God to give us the graciousness which will enable us to take the first step to put matters right.

Along with this phrase Paul puts another command. The Greek can equally well mean two things. It can mean: " Don't give the devil his opportunity." An unhealed breach, an unreconciled quarrel is a magnificent opportunity for the devil to sow dissension and dispeace. Many and many a time a Church has been torn into sects and factions because two individual people quarrelled, and let the sun set upon their wrath. It is well to remember that, when personal relationships deteriorate, the devil gets his chance, and he is not slow to take it. But there is another meaning which this phrase can equally have. The word for devil in Greek is *diabolos*; but *diabolos* is also the normal Greek word for a *slanderer*. Luther, for instance, took this to mean: " Give the slanderer no place in your life." It may well be that this is the true meaning of what Paul wishes to say. No one in this world can cause more trouble and do more damage than the slanderous tale-bearer. As Coleridge wrote in *Christabel*:

> " Alas! they had been friends in youth;
>   But whispering tongues can poison truth."

There are reputations murdered over the teacups every day; and when a man sees a tale-bearer coming, he would do well to shut the door in his face.

(iv) The man who was a thief must become an honest workman. This was very necessary advice, for in the ancient world thieving was rampant. It was very common in two places. It was common at the docks; and it was common above all in the public baths. The public baths were the clubs of the time; and stealing the clothes and the belongings of the bathers was one of the commonest crimes in any Greek city.

But the interesting thing about this saying of Paul is the reason which he gives for being an honest workman. He does not say: " Become an honest workman, so that you may reach independence and honestly support yourself." He says: " Become an honest workman, so that you may have something to give away to those who are poorer than yourself." Here is a new idea, and a new ideal— the ideal of working in order to give away. James Agate tells of a letter from Arnold Bennett the famous novelist to a less fortunate writer. Bennett was an ambitious and in many ways a worldly man; but in this letter, he writes to this fellow writer, whom he hardly knew except by name, and he says: " I have just been looking at my bankbook; and I find that I have a hundred pounds which I don't need; I am sending you a cheque herewith for that amount." There are demands on all of us, and in a modern society no man has overmuch to give away; but we do well to remember the Christian ideal of work, the ideal that we work, not to amass things, but to be able, if need be, to give them away.

(v) Paul goes on to forbid all foul-mouthed speaking; and then he goes on to put the same thing positively. He tells the Christian so to speak that his every word will do other people good. The Christian should be characterized by words which help his fellow men. As Moffatt translates it, Eliphaz the Temanite paid Job a tremendous compliment. " Your words," he said, " have kept men on their feet " (*Job* 4: 4). Such are the words that every Christian ought to speak.

(vi) Paul urges us not to grieve the Holy Spirit. The Holy Spirit is the guide and the director of life. When we act contrary to the advice and the warning and the counsel of our parents when we are young, we hurt them and we grieve their hearts. Even so, to act contrary to the guidance and the direction of the Holy Spirit is to grieve the Spirit and to hurt the heart of God, the Father, who, through the Spirit, sent His word to us.

THINGS WHICH MUST BE BANISHED FROM LIFE

Ephesians 4: 25-32 (*continued*)

PAUL ends this chapter with a list of things, one after the other, which must go from life.

(*a*) There is *bitterness* (*pikria*). The Greeks defined this word as *long-standing resentment*, as the spirit which refuses to be reconciled. So many of us have a way of nursing our wrath to keep it warm, of brooding over the insults and the injuries and the slights which we have received. The more we think of these things, the deeper rooted they will become. Every Christian might well pray that God would teach him how to forget.

(*b*) There are *outbreaks of passion* (*thumos*) and *long-lived anger* (*orgē*). The Greeks defined *thumos* as the kind of anger which is like the flame which comes from straw. It quickly blazes up and just as quickly subsides. On the other hand, they described *orgē* as anger which has become habitual and inveterate. To the Christian the burst of temper, and the long-lived anger are both alike forbidden.

(*c*) There is *loud talking* and *insulting language*. A certain famous preacher tells how his wife used to advise him in the pulpit, " Keep your voice down." Whenever we realize in any discussion or argument that our voice is raised, it is time to stop. The Jews spoke about what they called " the sin of insult," and they held that God does not hold the man guiltless who speaks insultingly to his brother man. Lear said of Cordelia:

> " Her voice was ever soft,
> Gentle and low, an excellent thing in woman."

It would save a great deal of heartbreak in this world, if we simply learned to keep our voices down, and if, when we had nothing good to say to a person, we did not say anything at all. The argument which has to be supported in a shout is no argument at all; and the dispute which has to be conducted in insults is not an argument, but a brawl.

So Paul comes to the summing up of all his advice. He tells us to be *kind* (chrēstos). The Greeks defined this quality as the disposition of mind which thinks as much of its neighbour's affairs as it does of its own. Kindness is as concerned with the feelings of other people, as it is with its own feelings. It is as concerned with the sorrows, the struggles, the problems of other people, as it is with its own. Kindness has learned the secret of looking outwards all the time, and not inwards. He tells us to forgive others as God forgave us. So, in one sentence, Paul lays down the law of personal relationships—and that law is that we should treat others as Jesus Christ has treated us.

THE IMITATION OF GOD

Ephesians 5: 1-8

You must become imitators of God, as well loved children imitate their father. You must live in love, as Christ loved you, and gave Himself to God as a sacrifice and an offering, a sacrifice which was the odour of a sweet savour to God. Let no one even mention fornication and unclean living and insatiable desire among you—it does not befit God's consecrated people to talk about things like that. Let no one even mention shameful conduct. Let there be no foolish talking and graceless jesting among you—for these things are not fitting for people like you. But rather let your talk be a gracious thanksgiving to God

> You know this and you are well aware of it, that no fornicator, no unclean liver, no one who gives rein to insatiate desire—which is idolatry—has any share in the kingdom of Christ and God. Let no one deceive you with empty words. It is because of these vices that the wrath of God comes upon the children of disobedience. Don't become partners with them.

PAUL sets before his Christian people the highest standard in all the world. He tells them that they must be imitators of God. Later Clement of Alexandria was to say daringly that the true Christian wise man practises being God. When Paul talked of imitation he was using language which the wise men of Greece could understand. *Mimēsis, imitation*, was a main part in the training of an orator. The teachers of rhetoric declared that the learning of oratory depended on three things—theory, imitation and practice. The main part of their training was the study and the imitation of the masters who had gone before. It is as if Paul said: " If you were to train to be an orator, you would be told to imitate the masters of speech; you are not training in oratory; you are training in life; and you must set yourself to imitate the Lord of all good life."

That imitation was to be above all in one direction. The Christian must imitate the love and the forgiveness of God. Paul uses a typical Old Testament phrase. He talks of the " odour of a sweet savour." This phrase goes back to a very old idea, an idea that is as old as sacrifice itself. When a sacrifice was offered on an altar, the odour of the burning meat went up to heaven, and the god to whom the sacrifice was offered was supposed to feast upon that odour. A sacrifice which had the odour of a sweet savour was a sacrifice which was specially pleasing and specially acceptable to the god to whom it was offered. Paul takes the old phrase which time had hallowed—it occurs almost fifty times in the Old Testament—and he uses it of the sacrifice that Jesus brought to God. The sacrifice of Jesus was well-pleasing to God; it was a sacrifice in which God took delight. And what was that sacrifice? The sacrifice of Jesus was a life of perfect obedience to God, and of perfect love to men, an obedience which was so absolute and a love which was so infinite that they accepted the Cross. What Paul says is: " Imitate God. And if you wish to imitate God and to imitate the sacrifice which Jesus made, you can only do so by loving men with the same sacrificial love with which Jesus loved them, and forgiving them in love as God has done." It is Paul's plea that the Christian must reproduce God's attitude of love and kindness and forgiveness and mercy in his own life.

Then Paul goes on to another matter. It has been said that chastity was the one new virtue which Christianity introduced into this world. It is certainly true that the ancient world regarded sexual immorality so lightly that it was no sin at all. It was the expected thing that a man should have a mistress. In places like Corinth the great temples were staffed by hundreds of priestesses who were sacred prostitutes, and whose earnings went to the upkeep of the Temple. In his speech *Pro Caelio* Cicero pleads: " If there is anyone who thinks that young men should be absolutely forbidden the love of courtesans, he is indeed extremely severe. I am not able to deny the principle that he states. But he is at variance not only with the licence of what our own age allows, but also from the customs and concessions of our ancestors. When indeed was this not done? When did anyone ever find fault with it? When was such permission denied? When was it that that which is now lawful was not lawful?" Cicero is saying that no Roman in his senses would forbid a young man to consort with prostitutes. The thing which best of all illuminates the point of view of the ancient world is this. The Greeks themselves said that Solon was the first person to allow the introduction of prostitutes into Athens and then the building of brothels; and with the profits of the new trade a new Temple was built to Aphrodite, the goddess of love. Nothing could show the Greek point of view better than the fact that the Greeks saw nothing wrong in building a temple to the gods with the proceeds and the profits of prostitution. When Paul set this stress on moral purity, he was erecting a standard which the ordinary heathen had never dreamed of. That is why he pleads with them so earnestly, and lays down his laws of purity with such stringency. We must remember out of what kind of a society these Christian converts had come; we must remember with what kind of a society they were encompassed. There is nothing in all history like the moral miracle which Christianity wrought.

JESTING ABOUT SIN

Ephesians 5: 1-8 (*continued*)

WE must note two other warnings which Paul gives.

(i) He says that these shameful sins are not even to be talked about. He says that they are not to become a subject for foolish talking and graceless jesting. The Persians had a rule, so Herodotus tells us, by which " it was not even allowed to speak such things as it was not allowed to do." To talk about a thing, to jest about a thing, to make it a frequent subject of conversation is to introduce it into the mind, and to bring nearer the actual doing of it. It is Paul's belief and warning that there are some things which it is not safe even to talk or to jest about. They should be banished from the Christian life. It is still a grim commentary on human nature that many a book and many a play and many a film has had a success simply because it dealt with subjects which are connected with the forbidden and the ugly things.

(ii) He says that his converts must not allow themselves to be deceived with empty words. What does he mean by that? There were voices in the ancient world, and even voices in the Christian Church, which taught men to think lightly of bodily sin. In the ancient world there was a line of thought called Gnosticism. Gnosticism began with a basic fact. It began from the contention that spirit alone is good, and that matter is always flawed and evil, that matter is essentially and in its very nature an evil thing. If that be so, it follows that only spirit is to be valued, and that matter must be completely and utterly despised. Now a man is composed of two parts; he is *body* and *spirit*. On this point of view only his spirit matters; his body is of no importance whatsoever. Therefore, some at least of the Gnostics went on to argue, it does not matter what a man does with his body. It will make no difference if he gluts and sates its desires. The body is completely unimportant. In a short time a man will be finished with it; only his spirit matters. These Gnostics therefore argued that bodily and sexual sin were of no importance because they were of the body and not of the spirit. Christianity met such teaching by the contention that body and soul are equally important, that God is the creator of both, that Jesus Christ for ever sanctified our human body by taking it upon Himself, that the body too is the temple of the Holy Spirit, and that Christianity is concerned with the salvation of the whole man, body, soul and spirit.

(iii) That was an attack which came from outside the Church; but there was an even more dangerous attack which came from inside the Church. There were those in the Church who perverted the doctrine of grace. We hear the echoes and undertones of Paul's argument with them in *Romans* 6. Their argument ran like this. " Do you say that God's grace is the greatest thing in all the world? " " Yes." " Do you say that God's grace is wide enough to cover every fault and sin and stain? " " Yes." " Then, if that be so, let us go on sinning, for God's grace can wipe out every sin. Nay, more—the more we sin the more chances God's grace will get to operate. Our sin is a good thing, for it produces grace which you claim is the greatest thing in the world." Christianity met that argument by insisting that grace was not only a privilege and a gift; it was a responsibility and an obligation. It was true that God's love could and would forgive; but the very fact that God loves us lays on us the obligation to deserve that love.

The gravest disservice that any man can do to a fellow man is to make him think lightly of sin. Any teaching which belittles the horror and the terror of sin is poisonous teaching. Paul besought his converts not to be led away and deceived with those empty words which took the terror and the sting from the idea of sin.

THE CHILDREN OF LIGHT

Ephesians 5: 9-14

> For once you were darkness, but now you are light in the Lord. You must behave as children of the light, for the fruit of light consists in all benevolence, and righteousness and truth. You must decide what is well-pleasing to the Lord. You must take no share in the barren works of the dark. Rather you must expose them, for it is a shameful thing even to speak about the hidden things which are done in secret by such men. Whatever is exposed to the light is illuminated. And everything which is illuminated becomes light. That is why it says: "Wake, O sleeper, and rise from the dead, and Christ will shine upon you."

PAUL saw the heathen life as life in the dark; and the Christian life as life in the light. So vividly does he wish to put this that he does not say that the heathen are children of the dark, and the Christians children of the light; he says that the heathen *are* dark and the Christians *are* light. Here Paul has certain things to say about the light which Jesus Christ brings to men.

(i) The light produces good fruit. It produces benevolence, righteousness and truth. Benevolence (*agathōsunē*) is a certain generosity of spirit. The Greeks themselves defined righteousness (*dikaiosunē*) as " giving to men and to God that which is their due." Truth (*alētheia*) is not in New Testament thought simply an intellectual thing to be grasped with the mind. The truth is moral truth;

it is not only something to be *known*; it is something to be *done*. The light which Christ brings makes us useful and helpful citizens of this world; it makes us men and women who never fail in duty, human or divine; it makes us strong to do that which we know is true. A tree will be fruitless unless the light of the sun can get at it; and a life will be fruitless unless the light of Christ touches it.

(ii) The light enables us to discriminate between that which is well-pleasing and that which is not pleasing to God. It is in the light of Christ that all motives and all actions must be tested. In the east the shops in the bazaars are simply little covered enclosures with no windows. Often a man might wish to buy a piece of silk or an article of beaten brass. Before he bought it he would take it out to the street and hold it up to the sun, that the light might reveal any flaws which happened to be in it. He would only purchase it, if it stood the test of the light. It is the Christian's duty to expose every action, every decision, every motive to the light of Christ. It is in that light that we must judge everything in life.

(iii) The light exposes that which is evil. Over and over again the best way to rid society or the world of any evil is to drag it out into the light. So long as the thing was being done in secret, it went on; but when it was dragged out into the light of day, it died a natural death. The surest way to cleanse the depths of our own hearts, and to cleanse the practices of any society in which we may happen to be involved, is to expose them to the light of Christ.

(iv) Finally, Paul has a wonderful idea about light. He says: " Everything which is illuminated becomes light." That is a difficult sentence. But what Paul seems to mean is that light has in itself a cleansing quality. In our own generation we know how it is a fact that many a disease has been conquered simply by letting the sunlight in. We know to-day about the healing that is in the rays of the sun. The light of Christ is like that. We must never think of the light of Christ as only a condemning and a cruel thing; it is a healing thing too. That which is set in the light of Christ is not only illuminated; it is also cleansed.

Paul finishes this passage with a quotation which is in poetry. In Moffatt's translation it runs:

" Wake up, O sleeper, and rise from the dead;
So Christ will shine upon you."

Paul introduces that quotation as if everybody knew it, but no one now knows where it came from. There are certain interesting suggestions. Almost certainly, being in poetry, it is a fragment of an early Christian hymn. It may well have been a part of a baptismal hymn. We must again remember that in the early Church nearly all baptisms were adult baptisms; they were baptisms of people who were confessing their faith, and who were coming out of heathenism into Christianity. As they arose from the water, it may well be that these were the lines which were sung, to symbolize the emergence of the new Christian from the dark sleep of paganism into the radiant and awakened life of the Christian way. Again, it has been suggested that these lines are part of a hymn, which was supposed to give the summons of the archangel when the last trumpet sounded over the earth. Then would be the great awakening when men rose from the sleep of death to receive the eternal life of Christ. These things are speculations, but it seems certain that when we read these lines, we are reading a little fragment of one of the first hymns the Christian Church ever sang.

THE CHRISTIAN FELLOWSHIP

Ephesians 5: 15-21

Be very careful how you live. Do not live like unwise men, but like wise men. Use your time with all economy for these are evil days. That is the reason why you must not be senseless, but you must understand what the will of God is. Do not get drunk with wine—that is profligacy—but be filled with the

> Spirit. Speak to each other in psalms and hymns and songs the Spirit teaches you. Let the words and the music of your praise to God come from your heart. Give thanks for all things at all times to God the Father in the name of our Lord Jesus Christ. Be subject to one another because you reverence Christ.

PAUL'S general appeal finishes with an exhortation to his converts to live like wise men. The times in which they are living are evil; they must rescue as much time as they can from the evil uses of the world.

Then Paul goes on to draw a contrast between two kinds of gathering—a pagan gathering and a Christian gathering. The pagan gathering is apt to be a debauch. It is a significant thing that we still use the word *symposium* for a discussion of a subject by a number of people. The Greek word *sumposion* literally means a drinking-party. Once A. C. Welch was preaching on this text: " Be filled with the Spirit." He began with one sudden sentence: " You've got to fill a man with something." The heathen found his happiness in filling himself with wine and with all the pleasures which are worldly pleasures; the Christian found his happiness in the fact that he was filled with the Spirit.

From this passage we can gather certain facts about the Christian gatherings in the early days.

(i) The early Church was a *singing Church*. Its characteristic was psalms and hymns and spiritual songs. The early Church had a happiness which made men sing.

(ii) The early Church was a *thankful Church*. Their instinct was to give thanks for all things and in all places and at all times. Chrysostom, the great preacher of the Church of later days, had the curious thought that a Christian could even give thanks for Hell, because Hell was a threat and a warning to keep him in the right way. The Christian Church was a thankful Church because its members were still dazzled with the wonder that God's love had stooped to save them; and it was a thankful

Church for never had men such a consciousness that they were in the hands of God. They were able to give thanks for all things, because they were convinced that all things came from God.

(iii) The early Church was a Church where men *honoured and respected each other*. Paul gives the reason for this mutual honour and respect; it was because they reverenced Christ. They saw each other not in the light of their trades or their professions or their social standing; they saw men in the light of Christ; and therefore they saw the dignity of every man; and mutual respect and honour were easy.

THE PRECIOUS BOND

Ephesians 5: 22-33

Wives, be subject to your husbands as to the Lord; for the husband is the head of the wife, even as Christ is the head of the Church, though there is this great difference, that Christ is the Saviour of the whole body. But, even allowing for this difference, even as the Church is subject to Christ, so wives must be subject to their husbands in everything. Husbands, love your wives, even as Christ loved the Church and gave Himself for the Church, that by the washing of water He might purify her and consecrate her as she made confession of her faith, that He might make the Church to stand in His presence in all her glory, without any spot which soils, or any wrinkle which disfigures, or any such imperfection, but that she might be consecrated and blameless. So ought husbands to love their wives, to love them as they love their own bodies. He who loves his wife really loves himself. For no one ever hated his own flesh; rather he nourishes it and cherishes it. So Christ loves the Church because we are parts of His body. For this cause a man will leave his father and his mother and will cleave to his wife, and the two will become one flesh. This is a symbol which is very great—I mean when it is seen as a symbol of the relationship between Christ and the Church. However that may be, let each and every one of you love his wife as he loves himself, and let the wife reverence her husband.

No one reading this passage in the twentieth century can fully realize how great it is. Throughout the years the Christian view of marriage has come to be accepted. Even if practice has fallen very far short of the ideal, the ideal has always been in the minds and hearts of men who live in a Christian situation. Marriage is regarded as the perfect and lifelong union of body, mind and spirit, between a man and a woman. But things were very different when Paul wrote. In this passage Paul is setting before men and women an ideal which shone with a radiant purity in an immoral world. A. W. Verrall, the great classical scholar, once said that one of the chief diseases of which ancient civilization died was a low view of woman.

Let us look briefly at the situation against which Paul wrote this passage and laid down this idea.

The Jews had a low view of women. In the Jewish form of morning prayer there was a sentence in which a Jewish man every morning gave thanks that God had not made him " a Gentile, a slave or a woman." The thing which vitiated all Jewish law regarding women was that in Jewish law a woman was not a person, but a thing. She had no legal rights whatsoever; she was absolutely in her husband's possession to do with as he willed. In theory the Jew had the highest ideal of marriage. The Rabbis had their sayings. " Every Jew must surrender his life rather than commit idolatry, murder or adultery." " The very altar sheds tears when a man divorces the wife of his youth." But the fact was that in the time of the Church, divorce had become tragically easy. The law of divorce is summarized in *Deuteronomy* 24: I. " When a man hath taken a wife and married her, and it come to pass that she find no favour in his sight because he hath found some uncleanness in her, let him write her a bill of divorcement, and send her out of his house." Obviously everything turns on the interpretation of the phrase *some uncleanness*. The stricter Rabbis, headed by the famous Shammai, held that that phrase meant adultery and adultery alone, and declared that even if a wife was as mischievous as Jezebel a husband might not divorce her except for adultery. The more liberal Rabbis, headed by the equally famous Hillel, interpreted this phrase in the widest possible way. They said that it meant that a man might divorce his wife if she spoiled his dinner by putting too much salt in his food, if she walked in public with her head uncovered, if she talked with men in the streets, if she spoke disrespectfully of her husband's parents in her husband's hearing, if she was a brawling woman, if she was troublesome or quarrelsome. A certain Rabbi Akiba interpreted the phrase *if she find no favour in his sight* to mean that a husband might divorce his wife if he found a woman whom he considered more attractive. It is easy to see which school of thought would predominate.

Two facts in Jewish law made the matter worse. First, the wife had no rights of divorce at all, unless her husband became a leper or an apostate or engaged in a disgusting trade. Broadly speaking, a husband, under Jewish law, could divorce his wife for any cause; a wife could divorce her husband for no cause. The woman was utterly helpless and defenceless under Jewish marriage law. Second, the process of divorce was disastrously easy. The Mosaic law said that a man who wished a divorce had to hand his wife a bill of divorcement. The document ran: " Let this be from me thy writ of divorce and letter of dismissal and deed of liberation, that thou mayest marry whatsoever man thou wilt." All that a man had to do was to hand that bill of divorcement, correctly written out by a Rabbi, to his wife, in the presence of two witnesses and the divorce was complete. The only other condition was that the woman's dowry must be returned.

In the time of the coming of Christianity even with

Judaism the marriage bond was in peril. So greatly was it in peril that the very institution of marriage was threatened, because Jewish girls were refusing to marry at all because the position of the wife was so uncertain.

THE PRECIOUS BOND

Ephesians 5: 22-33 (*continued*)

THE position was worse in the Greek world. Prostitution was an essential part of Greek life. Demosthenes had laid it down as the common and accepted rule of life: " We have courtesans for the sake of pleasure; we have concubines for the sake of daily cohabitation; we have wives for the purpose of having children legitimately, and of having a faithful guardian for all our household affairs." The woman of the respectable classes in Greece led a completely secluded life. She took no part in public life; she never appeared on the streets alone; she never even appeared at meals or at social occasions; she had her own apartments and none but her husband might enter into them. It was the aim that, as Xenophon had it, " she might see as little as possible, hear as little as possible and ask as little as possible." The Greek respectable woman was brought up in such a way that companionship and fellowship in marriage was impossible. A man found his pleasure and his friendship outside his marriage. Socrates said: " Is there anyone to whom you entrust more serious matters than to your wife—and is there anyone to whom you talk less? " Verus was the imperial colleague of the great Marcus Aurelius. He was blamed by his wife for associating with other women, and his answer was that she must remember that the name of wife was a title of dignity but not of pleasure. The whole Greek way of life made companionship between man and wife next to impossible. The Greek expected his wife to run his home, to care for his legitimate children, but he found his pleasure and his companionship elsewhere.

To make matters worse, there was no legal procedure of divorce in Greece. As someone has put it, divorce was by nothing else than caprice. The one security that the wife had was that her dowry must be returned. In Greece, home and family life were near to being extinct, and fidelity was completely non-existent.

THE PRECIOUS BOND

Ephesians 5: 22-33 (*continued*)

In Rome in Paul's day the matter was still worse. The degeneracy of Rome was tragic. For the first five hundred years of the Roman Republic there had been not one single case of divorce. The first recorded divorce was that of Spurius Carvilius Ruga in 234 B.C. But at the time of Paul, Roman family life was wrecked. Seneca writes that women were married to be divorced and divorced to be married. In Rome the Romans did not commonly date their years by numbers; they called them by the names of the consuls; Seneca says that women dated the years by the names of their husbands. Martial the Roman poet tells of a woman who had had ten husbands; Juvenal tells of one who had had eight husbands in five years; Jerome declares it to be true that in Rome there was a woman who was married to her twenty-third husband and she herself was his twenty-first wife. We find even a Roman Emperor Augustus demanding that her husband should divorce the lady Livia when she was with child that he might himself marry her. We find even Cicero, in his old age, putting away his wife Terentia that he might marry a young heiress, whose trustee he was, that he might enter into her estate in order to pay his debts.

That is not to say that there was no such thing as fidelity. Suetonius tells of a Roman lady called Mallonia who committed suicide rather than submit to the favours of Tiberius the Emperor. But it is not too much to say that the whole atmosphere of the ancient world was adulterous.

Chastity was the casualty of the increasing luxury of civilization. The marriage bond was on the way to complete breakdown.

It is against that background that Paul writes. When Paul wrote this most lovely passage he was not simply stating or restating the view that every man held. He was calling men and women to a new fidelity and a new purity and a new fellowship in the married life. It is the simple fact of history that no one in this world with the single exception of children, as we shall see, owes more to Christ than women. It is impossible to exaggerate the cleansing effect that Christianity had on ordinary everyday home life in the ancient world.

THE GROWTH OF PAUL'S THOUGHT

Ephesians 5: 22-33 *(continued)*

IT is in this passage that we find Paul's real thought on marriage. There are things which Paul wrote about marriage which puzzle and bewilder us, things which, if we are honest, we wish that he had never written. And the unfortunate thing is that it is these things which are so often quoted as Paul's view of marriage. One of the strangest chapters in all Paul's writing is I *Corinthians* 7. In that chapter he is talking about marriage and about the relationships between men and women. In that chapter the blunt truth is that Paul's teaching is that marriage is permissible in order to avoid something worse and for no other reason. " To avoid fornication," he writes, " let every man have his own wife, and let every woman have her own husband " (I *Corinthians* 7: 2). He allows that a woman whose husband had died may marry again, but it would be better if she remained single (I *Corinthians* 7: 39, 40). He would prefer the unmarried and the widows not to marry. " But if they cannot contain let them marry; for it is better to marry than to burn " (I *Corinthians* 7: 9). To put it crudely, the teaching of that strange and hurting chapter is that marriage is better than adultery, but that is all that can be said for it.

There was a reason why Paul wrote like that. He wrote like that when he was writing I *Corinthians* because he daily and hourly expected the Second Coming of Jesus, and it was therefore his conviction that no man and no woman should undertake any earthly ties whatsoever, but that they should all concentrate on using the short time which remained in preparing for the coming of their Lord. " He that is unmarried careth for the things that belong to the Lord, how he may please the Lord; but he that is married careth for the things of the world, how he may please his wife " (I *Corinthians* 7: 32, 33). When Paul wrote I *Corinthians* 7 he was really insisting that a man should love Jesus more than he loves father or mother or wife or child, that loyalty to Jesus should take precedence over the dearest loyalties of earth. And he was doing that because he believed that the Second Coming was to arrive at any moment.

But between I *Corinthians* and *Ephesians* there is a space of perhaps nine years. In these nine years Paul had realized that the Second Coming was not to be so soon as he had thought, that in fact he and his people were living, not in a temporary situation at the end of the world, but in a more or less permanent situation. And it is in *Ephesians* that we find Paul's true teaching on marriage, that Christian marriage is the most precious relationship in life, whose only parallel is the relationship between Christ and the Church.

If we are to be fair to Paul, it is from this chapter that we will draw his teaching on marriage, and not from the chapter in the earlier letter to the Corinthians. I *Corinthians* 7 contains crisis and emergency regulations at a time when Paul thought that the world had only days to exist. *Ephesians* gives us Paul's view of marriage as part of the permanent situation of the Christian life.

It is just possible that the *Corinthians* passage was coloured by Paul's personal experience. It would seem that in his days as a zealous Jew, Paul was a member of the Sanhedrin. When he is telling of his conduct towards the Christians, he says: " I gave my vote against them " (*Acts* 26: 10). Now it would also seem that one of the qualifications for membership of the Sanhedrin was marriage, and that therefore Paul must have been a married man. He never mentions his wife. Why? It may well be that it was because she left him when he became a Christian, and turned against him. It may be that when he wrote I *Corinthians* Paul was speaking out of a situation in which, not only did he expect the immediate coming of Christ, but in which he had also found his own marriage one of his greatest problems and sorest heart-breaks. It may be that at that time the circumstances of the world, as he saw them, and the circumstances of marriage as he had experienced them, made him feel that marriage was a handicap for the Christian. But it is certain that as the years passed on he came to see a relation-ship in marriage which was like nothing else than the relationship between Christ and the Church.

THE BASIS OF LOVE

Ephesians 5: 22-33 (*continued*)

SOMETIMES the emphasis of this passage is entirely mis-placed. Sometimes this passage is read as if the essence of it was the subordination of the wife to the husband. The single phrase, " The husband is the head of the wife," is quoted in isolation. But there is far more in this passage than that. The basis of this passage is not control; it is love. In this passage Paul says certain things about the love that a husband must bear his wife.

(i) It must be a *sacrificial* love. He must love her as Christ loved the Church and gave Himself for the Church. It must never be a selfish love. Christ loved the Church, not that the Church might do things for Him, but that He might do things for the Church. Chrysostom has a wonderful expansion of this passage: " Hast thou seen the measure of obedience? Hear also the measure of love. Wouldst thou that thy wife shouldst obey thee as the Church doth Christ? Have care thyself for her as Christ for the Church. And if it be needful that thou shouldst give thy life for her, or be cut to pieces a thousand times, or endure anything whatever, refuse it not. . . . He brought the Church to His feet by His great care, not by threats nor fear nor any such thing; so do thou conduct thyself towards thy wife." The husband is head of the wife— true, Paul said that; but he also said that the husband must love the wife as Christ loved the Church, with a love which never exercises a tyranny of control, but with a love which is ready to make any sacrifice for her good.

(ii) It must be a *purifying* love. Christ cleansed and consecrated the Church by the washing of water, on the day when each member of the Church took his or her confession of faith. It may well be that here Paul has in mind a Greek custom. One of the Greek marriage customs was that before the bride was taken to her marriage she was bathed in the water of a stream which was sacred to some god or goddess. In Athens, for instance, the bride was bathed in the waters of the Callirhoe, which was sacred to the goddess Athene. She was cleansed from impurity by the sacred water. It is of baptism that Paul is thinking. By the washing of baptism and by the confession of faith, Christ sought to make for Himself a Church, cleansed and purified and consecrated, until there was neither soiling spot nor disfiguring wrinkle upon it. Any love which drags a person down is a false love. Any love which coarsens instead of refining the character, any love which necessitates deceit, any love which weakens the moral fibre, any love from which a person emerges a worse person, is not love. Real love is the great cleanser and purifier of all life.

(iii) It must be a *caring* love. A man must love his wife as he loves his own body. He nourishes and cherishes his body, as Paul says. Real love always cherishes the one it loves. It loves not to extract service; it loves not to ensure that its own physical comfort is attended to; it loves not for its own convenience; it cherishes the one it loves. There is something wrong when a man regards his wife, consciously or unconsciously, as the one who cooks his meals and washes his clothes and cleans his house and trains his children. He must regard her, not as a kind of permanent servant, but as the one person whom it is his duty to cherish.

(iv) It is an *unbreakable* love. For the sake of this love a man leaves father and mother and cleaves to his wife. They become one flesh. He is as united to her as the members of the body are united to each other. He no more thinks of separating from her than he would think of tearing his own body apart. Here indeed was an ideal in an age when men and women changed partners with as little thought as they changed clothes.

(v) The whole relationship is, as Paul puts it, *in the Lord*. It is lived in the presence of the Lord; it is lived in the atmosphere of the Lord; its every motion is governed by the Lord; its every decision is taken in the Lord. In the Christian home Jesus is an ever-remembered, though an unseen, guest. In the Christian marriage there are not two partners, but three—and the third is Christ.

CHILDREN AND PARENTS

Ephesians 6: 1-4

> Children, obey your parents, as Christian children should. Honour your father and your mother—for this is the first commandment to which a promise is attached—that it may be well with you, and that you may live long on the earth. Fathers, do not move your children to anger, but bring them up in the discipline and the admonition of the Lord.

If the Christian faith did much for women, it did even more for children. It will always be true that in any civilization no one can help loving a child; but it will also remain true that in the pre-Christian and in the heathen civilizations there can exist a callousness and a cruelty which are impossible in a way of life in which the principles of Christianity have become supreme. In Roman civilization contemporary with Paul there existed certain features which made life perilous for the child.

(i) There was the Roman *patria potestas*, the father's power. Under the *patria potestas* a Roman father had absolute power over his family. He could sell them as slaves, he could make them work in his fields even in chains, he could take the law into his own hands, for the law was in his own hands, and punish as he liked, he could even inflict the death penalty on his child. Further, the power of the Roman father extended over the child's whole life, so long as the father lived. A Roman son never came of age. Even when he was a grown man, even if he might be a magistrate of the city, even if the state had crowned him with well-deserved honours, he still remained within his father's absolute power. " The great mistake," writes Becker, " consisted in the Roman father considering the power which Nature imposes as a duty on the elders, of guiding and protecting a child during infancy, as extend- ing over his freedom, involving his life and death, and continuing over his entire existence." It is true that the father's power was seldom carried to its limits, because public opinion would not have allowed it, but the fact remains that there are perfectly historical instances of a Roman father condemning his son to death and executing him. The fact remains that in the time of Paul the child was completely and absolutely in his father's power.

(ii) There was the custom of child exposure. When a child was born, it was placed before its father's feet, and, if the father stooped and lifted the child, that meant that the father acknowledged the child and wished the child to be kept. If he turned and walked away, it meant that he refused to acknowledge the child, and the child could quite literally be thrown out. There is a letter whose date is I B.C. from a man called Hilarion to his wife Alis. He has gone to Alexandria and he writes home on domestic affairs:

> " Hilarion to Alis his wife heartiest greetings, and to my dear Berous and Apollonarion. Know that we are still even now in Alexandria. Do not worry if when all others return I remain in Alexandria. I beg and beseech of you to take care of the little child, and, as soon as we receive wages, I will send them to you. If—good luck to you!—you have a child, if it is a boy, let it live; if it is a girl, throw it out. You told Aphrodisias to tell me: ' Do not forget me.' How can I forget you? I beg you therefore not to worry."

It is a strange letter, so full of affection, and yet so callous towards the child who may be born. A Roman baby always ran the risk of being repudiated and exposed. In the time of Paul that risk was even greater. We have seen how the marriage bond had collapsed and how men and women changed their partners with bewildering rapidity. Under such circumstances a child was a misfortune. So few children were born that the Roman government actually passed legislation that the amount of any legacy that a childless couple could receive was limited. Unwanted children were commonly left in the Roman forum. There they became the property of anyone who cared to pick them up. They were collected at nights by people who nourished them up in order to sell them as slaves, or to stock the brothels of Rome. These things are unthinkable nowadays, not because this is as yet a totally Christian civilization, but because Christian principles have gone so far to permeate western civilization that such things cannot be thought of.

(iii) Ancient civilization was merciless to the sickly or the deformed child. Seneca writes as if it was the commonest practice in the world, as indeed it was, " We slaughter a fierce ox; we strangle a mad dog; we plunge the knife into sickly cattle lest they taint the herd; children who are born weakly and deformed we drown." The child who was a weakling, or who was imperfectly formed, had little hope of survival.

It was in a situation like that that Paul wrote his advice to children and to parents. If ever it is asked what good Christianity has done to the world, we have but to point at the change in the status of women and of children, and the answer is undeniable and complete.

CHILDREN AND PARENTS

Ephesians 6: 1-4 *(continued)*

It is Paul's commandment to children that they should obey the commandment and honour their parents. He says that it is the *first* commandment. He probably means that it was the first commandment which the Christian child was taught to memorize and to know by heart. The honour that Paul demands is not the honour of mere lip service. The only way to honour parents is to obey them, to respect them, and never to cause them pain.

But Paul sees that there is another side of the question. He tells fathers that they must not provoke their children to wrath. Bengel answers the question why this command is so definitely addressed to *fathers*. Mothers have a kind of divine patience, but " fathers are more liable to be carried away by wrath." It is a strange thing that Paul repeats this injunction even a little more fully in *Colossians* 3: 21. " Fathers," he says, " provoke not your children to anger, *lest they be discouraged*." Bengel says that the plague of youth is a " broken spirit," the discouragement which can come from continuous criticism and rebuke and too strict a discipline. David Smith thinks that Paul wrote this out of bitter personal experience. He writes: " There is here a quivering note of personal emotion, and it seems as though the heart of the aged captive had been reverting to the past and recalling the loveless years of his own childhood. Nurtured in the austere atmosphere of traditional orthodoxy, he had experienced scant tenderness and much severity, and had known that ' plague of youth, a broken spirit.' "

There are three ways in which we can do injustice to our children.

(i) We can forget that things do change, that the customs of one generation are not the customs of another. Elinor Mordaunt tells how once she stopped her little daughter from doing something by saying, " I was never allowed to do that when I was your age." And the child answered, " But you must remember, mother, that you were *then*, and I'm *now*." Parents can do infinite damage by forgetting that times change and customs alter.

(ii) We can exercise such a control that that very control is an insult to our own upbringing of our children. To keep a child too long in leading-strings is simply to say that we do not trust him, and to say that we do not trust him, is simply to say that we have no confidence in the way in which we ourselves have trained him. It is better to make the mistake of too much trust than of too much control.

(iii) We can forget the duty of encouragement. Luther's father was very strict, too strict, strict to the point of cruelty. Luther used to say: " Spare the rod and spoil the child—that is true; but beside the rod keep an apple to give him when he has done well." Benjamin West tells how he became a painter. One day his mother went out leaving him in charge of his little sister Sally. In his mother's absence he discovered some bottles of coloured ink and began to paint Sally's portrait. In the doing so he made a very considerable mess of things with ink blots all over. His mother came back. She saw the mess, but she said nothing. She picked up the piece of paper and saw the drawing. "Why," she said, "it's Sally!" and she stooped and kissed him. Ever after Benjamin West used to say: "My mother's kiss made me a painter." Encouragement did more than rebuke could ever do. Anna Buchan tells how her grandmother had a favourite phrase even when she was very old: "Never daunton youth."

As Paul sees it, children must honour their parents; but parents must never discourage their children.

MASTERS AND SLAVES

Ephesians 6: 5-9

> Slaves, obey your human masters with fear and trembling, in sincerity of heart, as you would Christ Himself. Do not work only when you are being watched. Do not work only to satisfy men. But work as the slave of Christ, doing God's will heartily. Let your service be given with good-will, as to Christ and not to men. Be well assured that each of us, whether he is slave or free, will be rewarded by the Lord for whatever good we have done. And you masters, act in the same way towards your slaves. Have done with threats. For you well know that they and you have a Master in heaven, and with Him there is no respect of persons.

WHEN Paul wrote to slaves, he must have been writing to a very large number in the Christian Church. It has been computed that in the Roman Empire there were 60,000,000 slaves. In Paul's day a kind of terrible and fatal idleness had fallen on the citizens of Rome. Rome was the mistress of the world, and therefore it was beneath the dignity of a Roman citizen to work. Practically all work was done by slaves. Even doctors and teachers were slaves. Even the closest friends of the Emperors, their secretaries who dealt with letters and appeals and finance, were slaves. Often there were good masters, and often there were bonds of the deepest loyalty and affection between master and slave. Pliny writes to a friend that he is deeply affected because some of his well-loved slaves have died. He has two consolations, although they are not enough to comfort his grief. " I have always very readily manumitted my slaves (for their death does not seem altogether untimely, if they have lived long enough to receive their freedom); the other, that I have allowed them to make a kind of will, which I observe as rigidly as if it were good in law." There the kindly master speaks.

But basically and essentially the life of the slave was a grim and terrible life. In law a slave was not a person but a *thing*. Aristotle lays it down that there can never be friendship between master and slave, for master and slave have nothing in common; " for a slave is a living tool, just as a tool is an inanimate slave." A slave was nothing better, and had no more rights, than a tool. Varro, writing on agriculture, divided agricultural instruments into three classes—the articulate, the inarticulate and the mute. The articulate comprises the slaves; the inarticulate the cattle; and the mute the vehicles. The slave is no better than a beast who happens to be able to talk. Cato gives advice to a man taking over a farm. He must go over it and throw out everything that is past its work; and old slaves too must be thrown out on the scrap heap to starve. When a slave is ill it is sheer extravagance to issue him with normal rations. The old and sick slave is only a broken and inefficient tool. The law was therefore quite clear. Gaius, the Roman lawyer, in the *Institutes* lays it down: " We may note that it is universally accepted that the master possesses the power of life and death over the slave." If the slave ran away, at best he was branded on the forehead with the letter F which stood for *fugitivus*, which means runaway, at worst he was killed. The terror of the slave was that he was absolutely at the caprice of his master. Augustus crucified a slave because he killed a pet quail. Vedius Pollio flung a slave still living to the savage lampreys in his fish pond because he dropped and broke a crystal goblet. Juvenal tells of a Roman matron who ordered a slave to be killed for no other reason than that she lost her temper with him. When her husband protested, she said: " You call a slave a man, do you? He has done no wrong, you say? Be it so; it is my will and my command; let my will be the voucher for the deed." The slaves who were maids to their mistresses often had their hair torn out and their cheeks torn with their mistresses' nails. Juvenal tells of the master " who delights in the sound of a cruel flogging thinking it sweeter than any siren's song," or " who revels in clanking chains," or, " who summons a torturer and brands the slave because a couple of towels are lost." A Roman writer lays it down: " Whatever a master does to a slave, undeservedly, in anger, willingly, unwillingly, in forgetfulness, after careful thought, knowingly, unknowingly, is judgment, justice and law."

It is against that terrible background that Paul's advice to slaves has to be read.

MASTERS AND SLAVES

Ephesians 6: 5-9 (*continued*)

WE must note what Paul's advice to such slaves was, for here we will get the gospel of the Christian workman.

(i) He does not tell them to rebel; he tells them to be Christian where they are. Here is the great message of Christianity to every man. The message is that it is where God has set us that we must live out the Christian life. The circumstances may be all against us, but that only makes the challenge greater. Christianity does not offer us escape from circumstances; it offers us conquest of circumstances.

(ii) He tells the slaves that work must not be done well only when the overseer's eye is on them; work must not be done simply to please men. Work must be done in the memory that God's eye is on them and it must be done to please God. The conviction of the Christian workman is that every single piece of work he produces must be good enough to show to God. The problem that the world has always faced, and that the world is facing acutely to-day, is not basically an economic problem at all; it is a religious problem. We will never make men good workmen by increasing pay, or bettering conditions, or heightening rewards. It is quite true that it is a Christian duty to see to these things; but they in themselves will never produce good work. Still less will we produce good work by intensifying threats and increasing oversight and multiplying punishments and penalties. The only secret of good workmanship is that it is done for God. It is only when a man is taking all his work and showing it to God that work can be good.

But Paul has a word for masters too. His word for them is quite simple. The master of men must remember that although he is master of men, he is still the servant of God. He too must remember that all he does is done in the sight of and in the presence of God. And above all he must remember that the day comes when he and those over whom he was set will stand before God; and then the ranks of the world will no longer be relevant. They will both simply be men in the presence of God.

The problem of work would be solved if men and masters alike would both take their orders from God.

THE ARMOUR OF GOD

Ephesians 6: 10-20

> Finally, be strong in the Lord and in the power of His strength. Put on the armour of God, so that you may be able to stand against the devices of the devil. It is not with blood and flesh you have to wrestle, but against powers and against authorities, against the world rulers of this darkness, against malicious spiritual forces in the heavenly places. Because of this you must take the armour of God that you may be able to stand against them in the evil day, and that

you may be able to stand fast, after you have done all things which are your duty. Stand with truth as a belt about your waist. Put on righteousness as a breastplate. Have your feet shod with readiness to preach the gospel of peace. In all things take faith as a shield for with it you will be able to quench the flaming darts of the evil one. Put on the helmet of salvation. Take the sword of the Spirit, which is the word of God. Keep praying in the Spirit at every crisis with every kind of prayer and entreaty to God. To that end be sleepless in your persevering prayer for all God's consecrated people. Pray for me that I may be allowed to speak with open mouth, and boldly to make known the secret of the gospel, for which I am an envoy in a chain. Pray that I may have freedom to declare it, as I ought to speak.

As Paul takes leave of his people he thinks of the greatness of the struggle which lies before them. It is undoubtedly true that life was a much more terrifying thing for the ancient people than it is for us to-day. They believed implicitly in demons and devils and evil spirits. They believed that the air was filled with these evil spirits, all determined to work men harm. The words which Paul uses, powers, authorities, world-rulers, are all names for different classes of these evil spirits and demons. To Paul the whole universe was a battleground. The Christian had not only to contend with the attacks of men; he had to contend with the attacks of spiritual forces which were fighting against God. We may not take Paul's actual language literally; but from experience we do know this, that there is an active power of evil in this world. Robert Louis Stevenson once said: " You know the Caledonian Railway Station in Edinburgh? One cold, east windy morning, I met Satan there." We do not know what Stevenson's actual experience was, but we recognize the experience; we have all felt the force of that evil influence which seeks to make us sin. That is essentially what Paul means when he speaks about the demons.

So Paul musters his defence; and suddenly he sees a picture ready-made. All this time Paul was chained by the wrist to a Roman soldier. Night and day the soldier was there to ensure that Paul would not escape. Paul was in truth literally an envoy in a chain. Now Paul was the kind of man who could get alongside anyone; and beyond a doubt he had talked often to the soldiers who were compelled to be so near him. As he writes, he looks up; and the soldier's armour suggests a picture to him. The Christian too has his armour; and part by part Paul takes the armour of the Roman soldier and translates it into Christian terms.

There is the belt of truth. It was the belt which girt in the soldier's tunic and from which his sword hung and which gave him freedom of movement. Others may guess and grope; the Christian moves freely and quickly, because in any situation he knows the truth.

There was the breastplate. Righteousness is a breast-plate. When a man is clothed in righteousness he is impregnable. Words are no defence against accusations, but a good life is. Once a man accused Plato of certain crimes and sins. " Well then," said Plato, " we must live in such a way as to prove that his accusations are a lie." The only way to meet the accusations against Christianity is to show how good a Christian can be.

There were the sandals. The sandals were the sign of one equipped and ready to move. The sign of the Christian is that he is eager to be on the way to preach the gospel to, and to share the gospel with, others. He is always ready to take the news of Christ to those who have not heard it.

There was the shield. The word which Paul uses is not the word for the comparatively small round shield. It is the word for the great oblong shield which the heavily armed warrior wore. One of the most dangerous weapons in ancient warfare was the fiery dart. It was a dart tipped with tow dipped in pitch. The pitch-soaked tow was set alight, and the dart was thrown. But the great oblong shield was the very weapon to quench it. The shield was made of two sections of wood, glued together. When the shield was presented to the dart, the dart sank into the wood, and naturally the flame was put out. Faith can deal with the darts of temptation. With Paul, faith is always complete and perfect trust in Christ. That means that faith is always a close personal relationship with Christ; and when we walk close with Christ, we are safe from temptation.

There was salvation for a helmet. We must always remember that salvation is not something which looks back only. Salvation is not something which means only forgiveness for past sins; it means strength to deal with all future attacks of sin. The salvation which is in Christ gives us forgiveness for the sins of the past, and strength to conquer sin in the days to come.

There is the sword, and the sword is the word of God. The word of God is at once our weapon of defence and of attack. It is in the word of God we find at once our weapon of defence against sin, and our weapon of attack to fight the sins of the world. Cromwell's Ironsides fought with a sword in one hand and a Bible in the other. We can never defeat God's enemies or win God's battles without God's book.

Finally, Paul comes to the greatest weapon of all—and that is the weapon of prayer. We must note three things that Paul here says about prayer. (a) It must be constant. It must be at every time in life. It is maybe the greatest lack in the Christian life that our tendency is so often to pray only in the great crises of life. It is from daily prayer that there comes the daily strength of the Christian. (b) It must be intense. It must be sleepless and persevering. Prayer demands concentration. Limp prayer never got a man anywhere. It demands the concentration of every faculty upon God. (c) It must be unselfish; it must be for all God's consecrated people. The Jews had a saying, " Let a man unite himself with the community in his prayers." I think that often our prayers are too much for ourselves, and too little for others. We must learn to

pray as much and as intensely for others and with others
as for ourselves.

Finally, Paul asks for the prayers of his friends for
himself. And his prayer is not for comfort or for peace;
his prayer is that he may yet be allowed to tell God's
secret, that God's love is for all men, to all the world.
We would do well to remember that no Christian leader
and no Christian preacher can go on unless his people are
ever upholding his hands in prayer.

THE FINAL BLESSING

Ephesians 6: 21-24

> Tychicus, the beloved brother and faithful servant in
> the Lord, will provide you with all information, that
> you too may know how things are going with me, how
> I do. That is the very reason that I sent him to you,
> that you may know my affairs and that he may
> encourage your hearts.
> Peace be to the brethren, and love with faith, from
> God the Father and from the Lord Jesus Christ.
> Grace be with all who love the Lord Jesus with a
> love which defies death.

As we have seen, the letter to the Ephesians is an encyclical
letter, and the bearer of it from Church to Church was
Tychicus. Unlike most of his letters, Ephesians gives us
no personal information about Paul, except that he was
in prison; but Tychicus, as he went from Church to
Church, would tell the Christians how Paul was faring,
and would bring them a message of personal encouragement.

So Paul finishes with a blessing—and in it all the great
words come again. The peace which was a man's highest
good, the faith which was complete and trusting resting
in Christ, the grace which was the lovely and the free gift
of God—these things Paul calls down from God upon
his friends. And above all he prays for love that they
may know the love of God, that they may love men as
God loves them, and that they may love Jesus Christ
with an undying love.